"Using his lifelong training and personal experience combined with in-depth research spanning multiple cultures, faiths, and traditions, Antonio Pagliarulo clearly, honestly, and lovingly guides us through the origins and exercises of harnessing the energy of practical folk magic in our daily lives with his book *The Evil Eye*. Whether you are simply curious about what seems to be this rapidly rising pop-culture trend in jewelry and home decor or want to understand more about some traditions your friends and family observe and why, or whether you were raised knowing all about *malocchio, mal de ojo*, or 'bad juju,' this book is an indispensable addition to your library. It will quickly become your go-to reference guide in times of need, should you choose to delve deeper in practice and get in touch with your roots, spirit, and the magic that surrounds us. At the very least, learning how to observe the intentions, motivations, and emotional energies of others will help us become more in tune with ourselves and help develop priceless intuition and compassion toward the suffering of others, as well as our own."

—**Jessica Pimentel**, actor in *Orange Is the New Black*, and musician in *Brujeria* and *Alekhine's Gun*

"*The Evil Eye* by Antonio Pagliarulo is a remarkable work, being a book on one of the most important aspects of world magic by someone who is not only a good researcher but also a believer. The result is both a compendium of useful information for scholars and a manual of practical magic—and all the better for both aspects."

—**Professor Ronald Hutton**, author of *The Triumph of the Moon*

"A detailed, lively account of *il malocchio* from the point of view of a cultural insider thoroughly familiar with the tradition. Antonio Pagliarulo combines ethnographic observations and factual knowledge with magical expertise in a way that will appeal to practitioners from a variety of religious and esoteric traditions."

—**Sabina Magliocco**, professor of anthropology, University of British Columbia

"*The Evil Eye* by Antonio Pagliarulo displays diligent research into the subject, as well as how to protect yourself from the Evil Eye's malignant effects. Read this book and you will become a warrior and not a worrier. Envy is the Evil Eye: *l'invidia il malocchio*. The evil of envy is worldwide, the underside of vision! No need to write more. You who read my words, obtain this very valuable book."

—**Reverend Lori Bruno-Sforza**, HPS, Our Lord and Lady of the Trinacrian Rose Church and Chapel of the Archangel Michael

"I highly recommend Antonio Pagliarulo's contemporary exploration of this ancient and globally recognized yet persistently enigmatic subject viewed through the lens of his own culture and experience, as well as those of people from other cultures. His writing is approachable and relatable without skimping on the requisite academia. *The Evil Eye: The History, Mystery, and Magic of the Quiet Curse* is an excellent resource for anyone interested in folklore and folk magic."

—**Mary-Grace Fahrun**, author of *Italian Folk Magic: Rue's Kitchen Witchery*

"Combining the metaphysical understanding of an occultist, the research of a historian, and the first-hand wisdom of a true teacher, Antonio Pagliarulo dives deeply into the maladies, mysteries, and cures associated with the Evil Eye, including information ranging from the ancient world to modern popular trends. Even if you think you know all about the Evil Eye, I'm certain you will learn something new. I certainly did. And if you think of the Evil Eye as a superstition from a past time, you'll find out that it is still operating among us and how to protect yourself. Antonio brought clarity to some of the traditions of my own Italian Catholicism, and I'm deeply grateful."

—**Christopher Penczak**, cofounder of the Temple of Witchcraft and author of the Temple of Witchcraft series

"Having had the privilege of working with Antonio, I was given the ability to catch a small glimpse inside his craft as a practitioner of magic and as a writer. His ability to connect with his magic is as passionate and accurate as he is—a person who listens when the universe speaks. In his wonderfully and beautifully written book *The Evil Eye*, you will find a wealth of information and a thorough knowledge of magical workings. I do hope you enjoy this read as much as I did, and, like myself, will keep it in that special place in the library you visit often for reference."

—**Penny Cabot**, reverend and green minister, high priestess of the Cabot Kent Hermetic Temple

"Our eyes are among mankind's most powerful and ancient weapons. This belief is so widespread that cultures all around the world have words to name this weapon, such as Evil Eye, *mal de ojo, malocchio, matiasma*, and *xematiasma*. In *The Evil Eye*, Antonio Pagliarulo presents an informative, insightful, fascinating, and very important instructional book for understanding, handling, using, fighting, and defeating this powerful weapon. Ancient texts about this topic can be difficult to understand because they lack cultural nuances and are removed from lived experiences, but Pagliarulo with his vividly narrated stories brings this topic to today's readers in a digestible, entertaining, and straightforward way, making it the best book of its kind. *The Evil Eye* is a gem in the field of folklore, culture, and magic, and how they are intertwined. An exceptional contribution to treasure for future generations."

—**Laura Davila**, author of *Mexican Sorcery*, @daphne_la_hechicera

"Antonio Pagliarulo demystifies and brings new life to an age-old topic, the Evil Eye. A deep dive into the Eye's history and lore, his book explores why, how, and in what ways this energy has permeated multiple cultures. With an approachable understanding of magical workings, this book helps one recognize, protect, and cast spells and rituals that ward and work the Eye for the practitioners' own purposes. A must-have for spiritual and magical workers alike!"

—**Dawn Aurora Hunt**, author of *Kitchen Witchcraft for Beginners* and *A Kitchen Witch's Guide to Love and Romance*

THE
EVIL EYE

The History, Mystery, and
Magic of the Quiet Curse

ANTONIO PAGLIARULO

Foreword by Judika Illes,
author of *Encyclopedia of 5,000 Spells*

WEISER BOOKS

This edition first published in 2023 by Weiser Books, an imprint of
Red Wheel/Weiser, LLC
With offices at:
65 Parker Street, Suite 7
Newburyport, MA 01950
www.redwheelweiser.com

ISBN: 978-1-57863-797-3

Library of Congress Cataloging-in-Publication Data
Names: Pagliarulo, Antonio, author.
Title: The evil eye : the history, mystery, and magic of the quiet curse /
    Antonio Pagliarulo.
Description: Newburyport, MA : Weiser Books, an imprint of Red Wheel/Weiser,
    LLC, 2023. | Includes bibliographical references. | Summary: "This book takes
    a deep dive into the origins of the evil eye, from ancient Egyptian practices to
    those found in ancient Greece and Rome. Most people are unaware that the
    world's major monotheistic religions are replete with references to the evil
    eye. What did Jesus say about it in his Sermon on the Mount? The prophet
    Muhammad warned against the dangers of the eye, but what remedy did he
    provide to offset misfortune? Why and how does the evil eye appear in the
    rabbinic literature and other Jewish texts? These (and other) timeless questions
    are answered in this book"—Provided by publisher.
Identifiers: LCCN 2022056513 | ISBN 9781578637973 (Trade Paperback) | ISBN
    9781633412941 (Kindle Edition)
Subjects: LCSH: Evil eye. | BISAC: BODY, MIND & SPIRIT / Magick Studies |
    BODY, MIND & SPIRIT / Occultism
Classification: LCC GN475.6 .P24 2023 | DDC 133.4/4—dc23/eng/20221208
LC record available at https://lccn.loc.gov/2022056513

Cover design by Sky Peck Design
Takrut photo on page 89 by iStock; all other photos courtesy of Antonio
    Pagliarulo; all other images by Shutterstock
Author photo by Dana Maxson
Interior by Debby Dutton
Typeset in Weiss, Avenir LT, and OPTIBauer Text Initials

Printed in the United States of America
IBI
10 9 8 7 6 5 4 3 2 1

For Michael
With love

CONTENTS

FOREWORD

As the author of books devoted to witchcraft, I'm frequently asked to explain magic spells. What are they? Are they real? How do they work? My response is that magic spells are a conscious harnessing of magical energy in order to achieve a goal, but this inevitably leads to another question. What *is* magical energy? What exactly is the operating force behind a magic spell?

Magical energy is a naturally occurring current of energy that circulates throughout the universe, one that, if well cultivated, brings joy, empowerment, and all-around better living. In other words, although people create magic spells, the energy upon which these are based exists independently. This energy vibrates through virtually *everything*: colors, creatures, plants, us, you name it. This energy cannot be seen, heard, touched, or tasted. You will be aware of its existence by its effects. There is no single word for this energy in English—we must describe it, rather than name it—but that's not true for all languages: *ashé, baraka, mana,* and *qi* are but a few examples. The ancient Egyptians possessed a word—*heka* is the standard transliteration—and an origin story for this energy. According to one Egyptian creation myth, the Creator gazed out upon Creation, assuming it to be complete, only to realize that all was *not* good and that human beings, in particular, were destined for heartbreak. And so *heka* emerged as the final act of creation: a force created to help people ward off the inevitable harsh blows of fate.

I appreciate that this is an abstract concept that can be challenging, especially for those who find it difficult to acknowledge anything they cannot see, smell, touch, hear, or taste. For this reason, I typically contrast my explanation of magical energy with something harder to refute—nuclear energy, which also cannot be apprehended by the naked senses. It is known by its effects, which, to say the least, are too definitive to deny. Even as I write, the tools which Marie Curie used in her pioneering research into radioactivity remain too dangerous to handle.

Knowledge of nuclear energy is relatively recent. Though later acclaimed and eventually the first woman to win a Nobel Prize, during the early research period, Curie was the subject of such intense ridicule that she may as well have been attempting to prove the existence of magical energy. Her fellow scientists and many others refused to believe that radioactivity could exist, until it was proven beyond a shadow of a doubt. Implicitly, by using Curie's mysterious, hidden, luminous energy as a comparison, radioactivity is implied to be the antithesis of creative magical energy, but this is not accurate. The true antithesis to magical energy is the Evil Eye.

Magical energy is a neutral energy: what is done with it depends on the user. Angry people can consciously use magical energy to wreak destruction. However, this is not its primary purpose, as that Egyptian myth emphasizes. Magical energy is essentially a *creative* force that enables the spellcaster to achieve their desires and manifest (birth) something that did not previously exist, whether happiness, success, justice, or any other goal. The Evil Eye, on the other hand, is a destructive current of energy, a withering force that runs parallel to magical energy, which, as you will learn from this illuminating book by Antonio Pagliarulo, may be used to repel and combat it.

The term "Evil Eye" is capitalized, as it names a phenomenon: the eye as a weapon. The Evil Eye is most frequently, although not exclusively, transmitted via a glance. (A blind person can still transmit the Evil Eye.) The Evil Eye may be understood as akin to poison arrows, their target whatever sparks rage, grief, or jealousy. The Evil Eye's malicious energy shoots out through the eyes like weaponized glances, fueled by intense human emotion: envy, despair, awareness of inequity. Your eyes land on something that pains you to see. A quick glance at the news, your neighborhood, or even your family reveals what everyone knows: life is not fair. Why does someone else have what you desire but lack?

The Evil Eye is a withering force of sterility. Whatever it lands upon fails to grow and thrive, but withers away instead, whether this is luck, good fortune, health, well-being, pregnancies, virility, fruit trees, crops, children, animals, expensive purchases, or, in short, happiness and hope. The Evil Eye may be cast deliberately. It may be cast accidentally. It may also be cast involuntarily: sometimes the sender just can't help themselves and hence the need for constant vigilance and protection. The Evil Eye never sleeps. In the manner of the all-seeing Eye of *The Lord of the Rings* or some efficient and ubiquitous spiritual CCTV, you can never assume that you are not being observed. The Evil Eye is always scanning the world, seeking out happiness to crush and destroy.

How do you avoid the Evil Eye? How do you evade its glance?

Refrain from flaunting good fortune and utilize powerful amulets—the metaphysical equivalent of "speak softly and carry a big stick," the diplomatic axiom attributed to Teddy Roosevelt. (And if it's too late—if you've already been shot by the Eye or can't seem to shake off its effects, then please read on. Within these pages, Antonio Pagliarulo offers numerous rituals, tips, spells, and secrets to heal and ameliorate your situation.)

Evil Eye amulets take many forms, but a vast majority are anatomical. Most famous are those that are eye-shaped, such as the now ubiquitous *nazar*, colloquially known as "Evil Eye beads." Images of blue eyes are most frequent but that may be an indication of "othering." Although the Evil Eye is recognized virtually worldwide, its most famous and explicit expressions derive from Mediterranean regions, where brown eyes predominate and the blue-eyed glance is comparatively rare. This is ironic, as the phenomenon of the Evil Eye is anything but "other." None of us should feel removed from it. It's highly likely that everyone of us has, at least once, involuntarily transmitted the Eye and just as likely that each of us has been a victim, at least once.

Not all anti-Evil Eye amulets take the form of eyes. Images of hands ward off the Eye, serving as magical stop signs, while others are inspired by genitalia, whether explicitly, such as the winged phalluses of ancient Rome, or subtly, like Tuareg Ingall "crosses"—these images aren't meant pruriently but are instead intended to evoke the protective power of ancestors, as well as the life force: life over death, creativity over stagnation. Generative magic power counteracts the Evil Eye.

Ironically, for something so ubiquitous, the Evil Eye is a phenomenon that has received relatively little literary attention. When I first began writing about the Evil Eye in the very early 21st century, virtually the only books devoted to the topic were dry academic texts primarily focused on the activities, beliefs, and behavior of what the authors (mis)represented as uneducated and even "primitive" people. Recently, however, the Evil Eye has peeped out from the shadows where it once dwelt: Evil Eye-themed jewelry and amulets are now ubiquitous, sold in mall shops and by elite jewelers alike. There are even Evil Eye emojis.

Those often prohibitively expensive academic tomes have been joined by kitsch: books that present the Evil Eye as a quaint and even fun superstition.

Only now, however, with the publication of Pagliarulo's *The Evil Eye*, do we have a book that takes the Evil Eye seriously and offers clear, practical advice on identifying the Eye, avoiding, removing, and repelling it. *Finally*, there is a book written by an actual practitioner in plain language with warmth and compassion that takes the Eye and the misery it causes seriously. If you have been wondering about the Eye; if you fear it or think you have been struck by it; if you feel drawn to Evil Eye jewelry, this book is for you.

Let me offer one other piece of advice regarding avoiding the Evil Eye, one that does not involve amulets or magic but is no less powerful: be aware of others. Cultivate empathy and compassion for those around you. Remember, sorrows and dashed dreams are often kept secret. Be conscious of your good fortune and don't tempt the Eye.

May the words in Antonio's book help provide you with safety, relief, and happiness.

—Judika Illes, author of *Encyclopedia of 5000 Spells* and *Pure Magic: A Complete Course in Spellcasting*

INTRODUCTION

When I was a kid growing up in the Bronx, I didn't think there was anything unusual about my grandmother's kitchen. Pots were always simmering on the stovetop and the aroma of garlic and oregano permeated the air from dawn to dusk. What I remember most vividly was the curious arrangement on the counter beside the sink: a bowl filled with water, flanked by a spoon and a bottle of olive oil.

The water never found its way into the meals my grandmother prepared, but she gave that bowl a lot of attention. I often watched as she made gestures over it while whispering in her native Italian dialect. Only later did I learn that it was magic—not the sleight-of-hand seen on a stage, but the ability to effect change in real time. Armed with little more than water, a few drops of olive oil, and a secret incantation, my grandmother diagnosed and cured *il malocchio*—the Evil Eye—on a daily basis.

And *that* was no small feat.

I was raised in a largely ethnic, immigrant neighborhood where religion played a prominent role in everyday life. People went to church regularly and statues of the Virgin Mary dotted front lawns like trees. Spiritual practice should have been a cut and dry matter, but it wasn't. Faith and superstition shared the same narrow lane, and when they collided, it required more than a visit to the parish priest to solve the problem. This was especially true with the ever-present Evil Eye.

No one was immune to an envious glance or a disingenuous compliment. No area of life was beyond the Eye's reach. A birth, a marriage, a graduation, a new home, and a promotion at work were all fodder for jealousy. And when the Evil Eye struck, people panicked. Women like my grandmother were called to address problems that needed fixing fast—problems that didn't fall under the jurisdiction of liturgy.

Prayer is powerful, but it doesn't always yield immediate results. The effects of the Evil Eye, however, often come on swiftly and require equally fast action. Symptoms can be both physical and environmental. A minor symptom might be a headache or exhaustion, but a severe sign could include dizziness followed by a dangerous fall. People also called my grandmother after experiencing long spates of bad luck that had nothing to do with sickness: the car broke down twice, a pipe burst in the basement, then a wallet or purse got stolen.

It was the proverbial series of unfortunate events, and it didn't seem logical to believe that so many bad things could happen in rapid succession to one person or to a single family. But the litany of signs and symptoms wasn't as important as taking immediate action. If my grandmother found that malocchio was infiltrating someone's life, she quickly went about removing it. And, at the risk of sounding overly confident, it always worked.

Interestingly enough, despite this background, I didn't understand the Evil Eye's universality until I was a teenager. After nine years of solid Catholic education, I attended a public high school in Manhattan. It was a culture shock. I suddenly had friends who were Muslim, Baptist, Jewish, Zoroastrian, Hindu, Buddhist, and atheist. In short, for the first time in my life, I had friends who weren't just like me. My world got infinitely more interesting with other religions and customs to explore. I didn't talk much about my Italian heritage, and I believed wholeheartedly that my new comrades knew nothing of the rituals I had been raised with, *especially* those surrounding the Evil Eye. I was wrong.

Over the course of a week, usually while sitting in a noisy cafeteria, I learned that malocchio had many other names. My friend Joshua was Jewish; every time he talked about a good grade or something promising, he followed it with the Yiddish phrase *kinnehora*, which means "no Evil Eye." And then there was Rusa, a Zoroastrian, who told me that the gaze of a menstruating woman was particularly dangerous. Ali, whose parents had immigrated to the United States from Egypt, wore an *udjat*, an elaborate eye symbol the ancient Egyptians had painted on boats and coffins.

We each had a different name for the same thing. In very short order I came to realize that so many cultures not only had a unique historical link to this ancient and feared curse, but also rituals to detect and cure it. That realization formed the foundation of my life as a magical practitioner.

While my grandparents would never have considered themselves witches, they practiced folk magic, a very old and potent system of beliefs rooted in the mountains of their village in Campania, a region of southern Italy. It's a rich and varied tradition that offers magical solutions for every phase of life, from fertility spells to incantations that help carry a person's last breath into the next world.

Folk magic traditions differ tremendously from culture to culture; sometimes they even differ *within* the same culture. Factors like location and lineage contribute to the kind of magic that was (and still is) practiced. Some traditions are abundant with love spells, for example, and others focus primarily on protection.

But in the expansive universe of folk magic, you'd be hard-pressed to find a tradition that doesn't have at least one remedy for the Evil Eye. Whether you refer to it as *malocchio* (Italian), *mati* (Greek), *mal de ojo* (Spanish), or *ilaaco* (Somali), the Evil Eye stands at the crossroads where culture and magic meet. It is the common denominator of superstitions.

Those who eschew it as irreverent or irrelevant often forget that the Eye is mentioned in numerous sacred texts. In the Bible, it is referenced in the Gospel of Matthew, the Gospel of Mark, in the Book of Proverbs, and the Book of Deuteronomy. In *Bava Metzia*, a tractate of the Talmud (the Jewish compendium of law and legend), it is stated that among those buried in a cemetery, "ninety-nine of a hundred die from an *ayin hara* (Evil Eye)." In the Quran, verses 51 and 52 of the *Al-Qalam* are recited as protection against everything the Evil Eye represents: jealousy, malice, and misfortune. It is a widely held belief in the Hindu faith that a person's eyes emit the strongest energies of the body. Adherents of Zoroastrianism perform numerous cleansing rituals to ward away the Eye.

Interest in the Evil Eye has grown exponentially over the past few years and continues as it populates in mainstream culture. The "Evil Eye jewelry" people commonly wear is readily available in major retail outlets. The *nazar*—comprised of a series of concentric circles in hues of blue and white—is by far the most popular amulet used to ward away the Evil Eye, and it has moved out of the shadows and into the spotlight.

These days you can glimpse the *nazar* (as well as the *hamsa* and a few other protective charms) on dresses, shirts, purses, and shoes, not to mention pillows, plates, and bed sheets. It isn't strange to see a nazar hanging over a doorway in the foyer of someone's home or painted onto the backsplash of a modern kitchen.

Amulets to protect against the Evil Eye are also routinely spotted next to cribs and basinets. And don't forget the workplace. I've seen the nazar on more desks and in more offices than I can count.

Prevalent in nearly every culture, transcending time, boundaries, and enduring for millennia, the Eye is an abiding facet of the human condition. Even so, it is often the subject of confusion and misunderstanding. Can the Evil Eye strike anyone? How long does it last? Are there ways to remove it? This book answers those questions—and many others—and also explores some of the Evil Eye's fascinating history.

At the heart of the book, however, is magic. In these pages you will find a guide that has been designed to empower you psychologically, spiritually, and emotionally. Learning how to detect if the Evil Eye is afflicting you or your loved ones will heighten your self-awareness, strengthen your self-confidence, and intensify (if not entirely redefine) your own self-reliance.

Learning how to remove and banish the Evil Eye will deepen your relationship to the mystical because you'll experience first-hand the awe and ecstasy of magic; you are using prayer, ritual, or focused energy to heal yourself or someone else, and doing so will propel you further along the path of self-realization. Learning how to use the Evil Eye to defend yourself, protect your home and family, and safeguard your livelihood will diminish fear-based patterns and awaken in you a new fortitude with which to face life and its inevitable challenges.

Like magic itself, the Evil Eye does not belong to one culture or religion, and the spells and rituals in this book reflect its universal nature. You do not have to be a witch, shaman, or seasoned magical practitioner to use the methods contained within these pages.

That said, I have included spells, rituals, and prayers from many faiths—and from no particular faith—to maximize your personal connection to the process and the material. For example, you might choose to focus on the Catholic spells and rituals for a long time before feeling ready to explore the sections on Judaism, Islam, or modern witchcraft. You might also decide to stay with one or two rituals that are purely botanically based while gradually incorporating elements of the others into your practice. The choice is yours—and this book gives you many choices. By the time you reach the last page, you will be well educated about the Eye.

The ritual my grandmother performed was a closely guarded secret; it had been passed on to her by her own mother, a link in an unbroken, generational chain that continues even today. It was a privilege to grow up with the magic of tradition and the tradition of magic. Over the years I have steadily added to that well of knowledge as a practitioner, writer, and researcher. I've interviewed witches, healers, sages, and shamans from nearly every corner of the globe. Now it's time to share that wisdom.

This book is a complete course in Evil Eye magic, but it is also an amulet itself. Hold it, carry it, keep it on your desk or bedside table. Many of the prayers, spells and incantations within these pages are very old, and their power extends beyond space, time, and the printed word. In embracing this knowledge, you will stop *looking* at the world through the lens of fear and start *seeing* it from a place of power.

CHAPTER ONE

DEFINING AND DEMYSTIFYING THE EVIL EYE

If you ask five people to define the Evil Eye, you will likely get six different answers. That's understandable—it's a big topic with a long, colorful history. Numerous cultures and customs have been woven into the fabric of what is frequently referred to as "the Evil Eye belief complex." Historians don't always agree about its precise origins, but we know that the Eye goes back to at least 5,000 years BCE.

Time, however, has done little to mitigate its power.

The idea that a single glance can cause harm is alive and well today. In fact, many would argue that the belief has never been stronger given the Evil Eye's proliferation in popular culture. Amulets meant to ward away bad vibes are available in small occult shops and large retail chain stores alike. The most common of those amulets is the *nazar;* this ancient design has gone mainstream, from the fashion industry to the home goods market. It isn't just a piece of jewelry worn around the neck or wrist. You can spot the nazar hanging over doorways, on office desks, and even on pet leashes. But the evidence of the Eye's impact is far from topical.

Many religions are swift to condemn notions tied to magic and the occult, yet the Evil Eye is mentioned in several sacred texts. Most faiths have devotees who believe in the Eye despite dogma that instructs them not to. (Read on—you'll meet several of them.) This is hardly a surprise when we consider that fear, environmental and social upheaval, and uncertainty have become commonplace throughout the world. People want to feel protected and safe, and they want the same for their loved ones. All too often, however, religion fails to provide comfort for those who crave more than the rigid instructions given them by their clerics. Religion doesn't extend a kind hand to those who've had experiences that veer away from doctrine or liturgy, either. Words like *intuition* and *instinct* are frequently met with judgment, if not downright condemnation.

When organized religion is removed from the equation, we find that the desire for peace—in our homes and lives, as well as society in general—is the goal to which we all aspire. No one wants to walk around in a constant state of anxiety. No one wants to wonder if that new friend is really a foe. Sadly, however, we have all encountered a spate of bad luck or met someone who has made us feel uncomfortable. Have you seen the sharp flash of jealousy in the eyes of a trusted family member? Is that supportive co-worker—the one who's always cheering you on in staff meetings—*really* happy about your recent promotion? These experiences have nothing to do with religion and one need not have a connection to a particular spiritual path to believe in the Eye. In fact, many people who don't identify with spirituality on any level believe in it. Why is the Evil Eye so ubiquitous?

Because we know—viscerally—that it is real.

And yet, despite its universal nature, the Evil Eye remains steeped in misunderstanding and inaccuracy. Many people have a vague concept about "the look" but very few understand what it actually is.

Even fewer realize what it can do.

So what, exactly, is the Evil Eye? Is it a real energy or just an old superstition? Can anyone fall victim to it? What are its repercussions and how long do they last? Once afflicted, how does a victim break free of its negative clutches?

The Evil Eye is a baneful force transmitted through a stare or glance, and it can be delineated in three distinct ways. In the first, the Eye is accompanied by a compliment and/or praise. *You look beautiful. Congrats on the new job! It's so awesome that you've finally bought the house of your dreams!* The words sound nice, perhaps they even sound genuine, but the *feeling* behind those words is one of envy. That hidden emotion is supercharged energy—energy that is projected through the eyes and then absorbed by the unsuspecting target.

This particular manifestation of the Eye, rooted in malice or ill will, is the classic sugarcoated sting. The person giving the stare is fully aware of their emotions but can't (or won't) look at you and say, "It really irks me that you got engaged and are happy because I don't think you deserve to be," even though that's exactly what they're thinking. The jealous party takes the path of least resistance in order to avoid a confrontation. The compliment acts as a cloak, concealing the ugly truth of jealousy, anger, or greed.

Cowardly? Yes. Powerful? Yes—and perilously so. We can't always know the depths of that which is hidden. A person's envy for what you may have accomplished or acquired can be decades old; it's *their* festering emotional wound, yet it infects *you*. In most cases the victim doesn't perceive the praise as a ruse, and with their defenses down (or nonexistent), they become susceptible to psychic attack. The Bible sums it up neatly in a verse from *Song of Solomon*: "Jealousy is cruel as the grave." That cruelty feels particularly devious when someone chooses to look you straight in the eyes while showering you with false adulation. Makes you wonder—to what other lengths will their envy drive them?

The second way the Eye can afflict a person is much more direct and doesn't rely on the smokescreen method of attack. The emotions that bring about discord are fully present but not concealed by smiles, winks, and hollow praise. That confrontation I mentioned earlier? Here, the person who wishes you ill isn't concerned with consequences or discretion. They have one goal: to make sure that you understand and feel their dislike of you. The individual who holds you in such contempt is likely willing to make a public display of the matter. In this situation, you won't spend any time wondering who's harboring resentment toward you, nor will you second-guess whether the Evil Eye is at work in your life. The symptoms and signs will manifest swiftly given the combative nature of the circumstance.

Let's consider a fairly common scenario that illustrates this particular iteration of the Eye. You're currently in a happy relationship, but it took a bit of effort to get there because your partner has an ex-girlfriend who believes she was scorned. The ex is still lamenting her new status as a single woman and blames you for her heartache. One day, you run in to her unexpectedly at the supermarket. You spot each other from opposite ends of aisle five and she immediately locks her eyes on you. Her lips start to move and her gaze homes in on you with precision. She doesn't attempt to hide her feelings. In fact, she's blatantly hostile, muttering one unpleasant word after another. What you see in her eyes is hatred. It might not surprise you, but from a spiritual perspective it *does* put you in a dangerous place. The animosity that the ex has been holding in her mind for months is now the worst kind of weapon—one born out of anger, resentment, jealousy, and fear.

While you might perceive an encounter like this as little more than a brush with unpleasantness, it can, in actuality, harm you.

Why? Because a person who's willing to express their animosity for you literally vis-à-vis is brimming with pent-up emotion. Emotion is energy, and energy doesn't disappear—it only changes form. Think of jealousy and anger as a conjoined current rushing through a person's body; over time, that current solidifies into an arrow that's eager to find its target.

The target? You.

When you're in the sightline of hostility, the eyes become a means of both egress and access, and via that portal the Evil Eye is transmitted.

Interestingly, the third way in which the Eye manifests isn't quite as disturbing and doesn't hinge on a nasty person in your midst. The previous definitions had everything to do with malicious intent, but many cultures believe that an individual can unleash the Evil Eye *unintentionally*. A wealth of compliments or adulation—genuine though it all may be—can stir up negative juju even when avarice, envy, and greed are absent. This theory harkens back to the old adage that too much of a good thing will create something bad. Joy begets sorrow, laughter brings tears, an unbalanced scale eventually gives way—you've likely heard these aphorisms. What they all add up to is the collective belief that fate should not be tempted.

Consider the normal sequence of events that unfolds when you share good news about yourself with your family and friends. There's cheering, joy, pride, lots of pats on the back . . . and it eventually leads to more praise. *We always knew you would succeed! This is a testament to your intelligence! Hey, kid, you've definitely arrived!* Everyone is happy for you and the adulation feels intoxicatingly good, so much so that talking about your accomplishments becomes a habit. That's where things have the potential to get sticky. You have every right to be proud of yourself, but a repeated monologue about your life and its shiny new upgrade will bring negativity on to your path.

I grew up with this mentality but didn't understand it until I was a young adult. My mother and father immigrated to the United States from Italy and Argentina, respectively, bringing with them a long list of beliefs that ultimately shaped their perceptions about how the world worked. The power of the Evil Eye was undoubtedly at the top of that list. My siblings and I were taught early on to be careful about what we shared with others, whether it was an awesome birthday gift or news of an academic scholarship. Our silence had nothing to do with maintaining a sense of privacy among friends and neighbors. Rather, my parents and grandparents feared that in our excitement we would somehow appear boastful, and boasting about one's success or general happiness is a surefire way to rouse the Eye.

Here, when no ill will is present, the Evil Eye is a nebulous concept. There are people in your life you absolutely *know* would never wish you ill. And while you've been bragging about your good luck, you certainly didn't mean to turn that luck around. So, who gets the blame? Everyone and no one. Frustrating, yes—but not entirely illogical.

Think about the last time you noticed something that really caught your attention; it was likely too bright or too loud or just too damn distracting to ignore. It's much the same when it comes to the Evil Eye. Flaunting your good fortune or talking constantly about your splendid vacation plans can be acts of self-sabotage. When you brag, you are asking the Eye to look at you. And here's the big question: Will it see only what's in its periphery and then move on, or will it focus on your happiness and extinguish it with laser-like precision? More often than not, it's the latter.

Take an example from my childhood. When I was a kid, a pregnancy was *never* announced outside of immediate family members; it wasn't even discussed until the expectant mother was clearly showing. I remember my own mother's reaction whenever she received an invitation to a baby shower. She was confused.

She didn't understand why any woman would risk putting herself and her unborn child in the path of malocchio. To celebrate an event that hadn't yet occurred—especially an event as delicate as childbirth—was like standing directly in front of the Eye while waving a sign that read: *Look at me and how happy I am!* If ever there was a way to court danger, it was having a baby shower. Amid a flurry of joyful well-wishers were undoubtedly guests whose compliments concealed needles of envy and resentment. Why take the risk? The same was true of people who bought a new house. Tell Mom, Dad, and your siblings, but *don't* talk elsewhere about that lovely Victorian with four fireplaces until *after* you've signed every document and collected every key.

Incidentally, that brings us to the topic of inanimate objects. It's a fairly common belief that the Evil Eye is a malady for mortals. This, alas, is false. The aforementioned new house is subject to the ire of an envious stare, but so are cars, antiques, furniture, jewelry, clothing, the remodeled entryway, the refurbished kitchen, or any other prized possession. Envy doesn't discriminate. To a certain degree, an individual's success is defined—at least somewhat—by objects, but it isn't only the CEO and the wealthy widow who love their toys. We all have things that bring us joy and that we look upon with pride. Personally, I buy books as if I'm immortal. I have a friend who collects vintage watches. Have you ever met people who are so proud of their recent home renovations that they talk about nothing else? We form attachments to our personal possessions; they hold our energy and even provide clues to our identity. A person might well look past you only to focus on your car, your house, or the expensive bracelet glittering on your wrist. Sure enough, the Eye will strike. How many times have you heard someone lament an object's untimely demise? *Why did it break? I just bought the damn thing!*

It doesn't stop there: animals are also susceptible to the Evil Eye. In centuries past, envy was frequently blamed when animals fell ill, were injured, or died unexpectedly. Cattle, horses, goats, sheep, chickens—they were vital components of the agricultural cycle. The livelihoods of families—not to mention entire towns and villages—depended on livestock. The same was true for vegetation. If a crop wasn't bountiful, farmers were quick to see the land as blighted by the Eye. Today, we know that animals and plants alike suffer from any number of natural ailments, but it's not uncommon for pet owners to place amulets on the leashes and collars of their dogs and cats.

All that said, it's not my goal to frighten you into a life of measured silence. Nor does any of the aforementioned mean that you shouldn't share your blessings. Celebrations are necessary expressions of love, hope, success, hard work, milestones, and personal achievement. Everyone deserves a good long moment in which to shine. But to quote the late, great Maya Angelou: "There's a fine line between loving life and being greedy for it." That greed too often leads to arrogance. The key is to create a healthy balance of self-praise and discretion, which is accomplished by being mindful of your speech. And it isn't solely about talking. What are you posting on social media? Every platform exposes an aspect of your life, and every aspect of your life is a potential point of impact.

For many, the Evil Eye is a difficult concept to accept because it mirrors our deepest fear: that life can be shattered by something as simple as another person's glance or our own boastful ways. While the latter can be mitigated through self-discipline, the former is completely out of our hands. *Anyone* can look at you—it's an action that cannot be controlled. If you currently view the world as an inherently good place inhabited by people who want only to see you happy and healthy, I implore you to keep reading. What you'll find in these pages will inspire you to ask important questions about human nature, and the answers may redefine how you assess and manage relationships. You might also examine your own ideas about safety and what it really means. Even a cursory glance at our history—not to mention our present—paints a clear picture of the human capacity for cruelty. Jealousy, greed, and resentment are as much a part of the human heart as joy, compassion and love. A positive mindset is healthy, but it can also be toxic if it blinds you to the need for protection.

To be aware of the Evil Eye means to speak, act, and live wisely, with calm caution and informed strength. Understanding how the Eye works is about reclaiming ancient knowledge and using that knowledge in a way that enhances your life and the lives of your loved ones. No, you won't run around second-guessing every compliment. You won't develop habits that mirror paranoia, either. But you will certainly hone your abilities to distinguish a simple mishap from a negative energy pattern.

Above all, you'll come to realize that your modern life can benefit from old magic.

THE QUIET CURSE: AN INSIDIOUS DANGER

Curse. To most people, the word conjures disturbing images: bloodstained altars, handfuls of graveyard dirt, carcasses stuck with pins. If you have ever entertained the possibility that you might be cursed, a strand of your own hair is probably also on the list of nefarious ingredients. But the gory details comprise only a small part of the fear. What makes a curse truly frightening is the idea that someone can damage your life through occult knowledge and their own desire to use it against you. Here's the truth: someone can.

A curse, from the perspective of a magical practitioner, is an intentional work meant to deliver harm to a person or situation; it usually requires specific ingredients and the carrying out of specific steps. A practitioner who wants to curse his boss, for example, might spend a few days collecting the accoutrements that will fuel his magic: rusty nails, bits of broken glass, and the abusive boss's fingernail clippings. Then the practitioner must actually *cast* the curse. This is no small feat. The casting of a curse requires a tremendous amount of energy, concentration, and skill, not to mention proper timing; it's also emotionally and physically taxing. Other factors can include invoking or petitioning a particular deity and taking the necessary steps to ensure the magic won't backfire. In short, most curses are labor-intensive.

The Evil Eye, on other hand, requires nothing more than a glance. Forget altars, herbs, bones, and blood. Forget about arcane knowledge. The Eye doesn't need an incantation to fuel its power. Jealousy, envy, and resentment are universal emotions. You've felt them firing up your own blood and may have even acted on them in the past. You've also felt the backlash of another's jealousy and the unpleasant sting that accompanies it.

Right here, right now, in the privacy of these pages, think back to the last time you experienced a flash of jealousy. How did you react? Did you vocalize it? Did you admit the envy to anyone other than yourself? The answer to the last two questions is likely a resounding "No." That's perfectly normal. We're ashamed to express jealousy because doing so exposes both our insecurities *and* our desires—a double slap to the ego. When jealousy starts screaming inside of us, we tend to stay quiet.

Let's flip the coin. Can you recall a time when you were the target of jealousy? It's an awkward situation that results in partic-ular—and particularly ugly—feelings. If the offending individual was a friend or relative, you likely felt shock, disappointment, and anger the moment you realized their comment was disingenuous or their eyes too sharp. Even the envious glance of a stranger can bring about discomfort. Keep thinking about your own experi-ence for a moment. Did the jealous person approach you and unabashedly admit to wanting what you had? Probably not. It's more likely they went on coveting you or something you had in silence—a silence brimming with destructive energy.

A quiet curse.

The ability to cast the Evil Eye is inborn, not inbred; it belongs to every one of us. In fact, it's woven in to our very nature. The Eye's point of origin is emotion, and we will all experience feelings of envy, greed, and resentment at some point in life. Those feelings have a solid but silent trajectory, and when that trajectory finds its target, the quiet curse is unleashed.

Most people define the word *attack* through images of war and physical confrontation—bombs and missiles, bruises and blood. It's imperative to remember that not every attack is waged violently. Some attacks aren't even intentional. A person can cast the Evil Eye unknowingly if their envy is strong enough. A woman who has been unable to conceive can wish her pregnant friend well while simultaneously coveting the experience of pregnancy and motherhood. Over time, a visceral longing can become a bitter fury.

We can't control another person's thoughts or feelings. We can only control how we choose to inform and protect ourselves from harmful energy. When it comes to envy, we must always remember that the quiet curse has loud and brutal consequences.

THE EVIL EYE AT WORK

The summer of 2014 began auspiciously for Denise and Jack. Both forty, they had been married for six years and were settling in to the new home they had just purchased in a suburb north of New York City. The house, a big colonial on a tree-lined cul-de-sac, was a clear reflection of their success. It was, according to Denise, "a very lucky period" in their lives.

On the Fourth of July, the couple decided to have a small housewarming party. They invited close family members and only a handful of friends. Denise cooked up a storm and Jack made his signature martinis as guests strode from the sun-flooded living room to the large backyard. The event was a success on many levels.

But those good vibrations didn't last long. Early the next morning, Jack was awakened by a weird sound. He quickly discovered that the faucet in one of the upstairs bathrooms was leaking. That night, while preparing dinner, a hinge on a cabinet above the refrigerator broke. Several hours later, shortly after going to bed, he and Denise were awakened by a huge *boom* that "shook the house like a bomb." In the foyer downstairs, they found a chandelier on the floor surrounded by chunks of broken glass; somehow, it had come loose and fallen right out of the ceiling.

Jack was officially done shrugging off the incidents.

"My mind immediately went to the dark side," he explained. "I looked at Denise and said, 'We should never have had that damn party!' There was no doubt in my mind that we'd been hexed."

Denise, however, refused to even consider the possibility. "I waved him away and went to get a broom and a garbage bag," she said. "I was enraged that he had even brought it up. I told him to grow up."

In retrospect, Denise understands why her reaction had been so visceral. Raised in a traditional Irish-Italian family, she had left organized religion in her early twenties and had no intention of revisiting it.

"I grew up with superstitions," she explained. "Everything we did in my family was based on a belief that would either bring you bad luck or good luck, and it turned my mother into a basket case. For years I blamed every mishap in my life on forgetting to knock on wood or forgetting to spit whenever someone gave me a compliment. That damn Evil Eye was always watching. It took many years to overcome it, and I didn't want to go back to that craziness ever again."

Unlike Denise, superstition wasn't a part of Jack's childhood. As an undergraduate student, however, he spent a year abroad in Greece, where he immersed himself in the country's culture, including the belief in the Evil Eye. That another person's mere glace could make you sick or rattle your life initially seemed irrational to Jack. Eventually, however, the seeds of belief were planted and he left Greece a closet believer.

Over the years, Jack had thought about the Eye only a handful of times. Now, less than two days after their housewarming party, he was convinced it had struck him and Denise in a huge way. In addition to the broken chandelier and other mishaps, he started having intermittent headaches.

The headaches were compounded by a "heaviness" in the air that made Jack irritable and edgy. Suddenly the house felt "different" to him.

To Denise, however, the broken chandelier was "just a thing that happens every now and then." She cleaned up the glass and went back to bed. When she awoke a few hours later, it was to the sound of Jack cussing in another part of the house. She found him at the staircase landing, where several tiles had come loose.

"I knew it was strange," Denise said, "but I wouldn't admit it out loud. Who wants to admit that there could be a curse on their house? It brings up so many weird feelings and questions. Once you believe it, the next thing is thinking about how to get rid of it. My parents would have already said ten rosaries and called a priest. I didn't want to do that."

Over the next few days, Denise's reticence to believe in the Evil Eye was severely tested. Another bathroom sink started leaking, the garage door began to malfunction, and the basement had a small flood. The power went out twice, and on both occasions their house was the only dark spot on the street. Then, on a clear Friday night, a bird crashed into one of their bedroom windows; the sound was so sickening and the aftermath so gory, Denise vomited twice.

"It was out of hand," Jack said. "The house was in near perfect condition when we bought it and then all of this weird stuff started happening. It felt like a presence was sitting on the house, watching and waiting."

Barely a week after the party, Denise felt as though her life had been flipped on its head. She was scared of what might happen next. Now it seemed irrational to believe in anything *but* a supernatural source. A force had entered their lives—of that she had no doubt—and despite all of the confusion, she was able to identify what she believed was its true mission.

"Jack and I basically started and ended each day with a fight," she explained. "Every time something broke or failed, we turned on each other. One night I was standing at the window, feeling awful, and it just hit me—this thing that was staring at us and making us miserable . . . it wanted to break us up, to pull us apart. That was its main goal. It was using the house to get to us."

And the source of the *it?*

"I spent days doing my own research," Jack said. "I didn't think we had a ghost or a poltergeist or anything like that. But whenever I came upon the Evil Eye, all of the pieces fell into place."

It was the last conclusion Denise wanted to reach, but when she allowed herself to really think about it, without judgment or recrimination, it made sense. "Everything started happening *immediately* after we threw the housewarming party," she said. "Not a moment before."

Denise and Jack began seeking out answers. Neither of them was particularly spiritual at the time, so they didn't know where to look for help. Denise remembered the real estate agent who had sold them the house—he was a spiritual guy and had mentioned having spent time in a monastery. She reached out to him and he responded almost immediately.

"I was completely honest with him," Denise explained. "I didn't mask or mince words. As soon as I mentioned the housewarming party he said, 'That's the Evil Eye!' But then he asked if I had done anything beforehand to protect the house *and* me and Jack. That hadn't occurred to me because at the time I wasn't in that frame of mind. I didn't know you could ward away the Evil Eye or cleanse yourself of it."

The real estate agent led Denise and Jack to a metaphysical practitioner who lived ten miles away. The practitioner, an Italian-American woman, quickly diagnosed Denise and Jack with the Evil Eye and removed it with two rituals. She gave Denise and Jack an amulet to hang above the front door of their house: a nazar, the traditional charm used to ward away the Eye. The practitioner also instructed them to keep one in their bedroom.

"I can tell you the exact date when the practitioner called to tell us that she had removed the negativity from our lives because I wrote it down," Denise said. "That day, when I got home from work, I went on the back deck and kind of held my breath. But then a feeling settled over me, a calmness that I hadn't felt in a while. I was able to see the things I used to notice before all the chaos started—the rose garden, the butterflies. I just felt like I was able to take a deep breath again, if that makes sense."

Jack noticed a shift soon after he heard that the ritual to banish the Evil Eye had been done. "I was standing in the driveway unloading groceries from the car when one of our neighbors walked by," he explained. "The guy was walking his dog. He told me that Denise and I had done a beautiful job repaving the front walkway. The compliment came as a surprise, but I took it as a good sign, and I was right."

Jack's intermittent headaches stopped. For the next few days he and Denise went about their lives quietly. There were no incidents in the house, and they didn't have a single fight. The balance had been restored. The impact of the experience, however, has endured.

"I approach everything with a lot more caution," Denise explained. "I guess you could say I'm less trusting of people than I used to be, even those who are closest to me. Do I know who gave us the Evil Eye? Do I know the identity of the person or people who were envious of our success? No, but in a way, that's not as important as knowing how to protect yourself and your family. I'm not a fanatic about getting the Evil Eye, but I'm definitely aware of it, and I believe that awareness gives me a certain level of safety."

FIRE IN THE EYE: SIGHT, SCIENCE, AND THE POWER OF A STARE

A few years ago, my friend and I were guests at a wedding. In the middle of the festivities, he tapped my shoulder and said: "Someone across the room is giving me *u'malocchio*. I can feel her doing it—it's like two hot laser beams are shooting right out of her eyes!"

That image, while humorous, isn't the stuff of fiction. There was a time in the history of vision science when it was believed that sight happened via *extramission*—a process by which beams of light radiate from the eyes to form a person's field of vision. In this line of thought, those beams possess a sentient quality, like tendrils that reach out and "touch" whatever they focus on.

Sound odd? Among those who supported the theory were Plato, Ptolemy, and Euclid. Empedocles correlated eyes to lanterns, infused with a kind of mystical radiance attributed to the goddess Aphrodite. Have you ever seen a cat's eyes gleaming in darkness? That otherworldly glow was considered proof of the fiery emanation that enabled sight. Hence, fire in the eyes.

Around 100 CE, the Greek philosopher Plutarch wrote *Symposiacs*, in which he stated that the mysterious rays emitted by human eyes were powerful enough to kill young children and small animals. The Greek poet Heliodorus of Emesa was also a proponent of extramission. In his work *Aethiopica*, he wrote: "When anyone looks at what is excellent with an envious eye, he fills the surrounding atmosphere with a pernicious quality, and transmits his own envenomed exhalations into whatever is nearest to him."

But the theory of extramission didn't hold. If the eyes possessed such a fiery power, why couldn't people see in the dark? If the beams darting from a person's eyes were expansile, shouldn't far away objects be just as visible as those that are near? Such questions led Aristotle (among others) to pose and ultimately favor the theory of *intromission*—that certain rays of light were transmitted *from* objects and *to* the eyes, which creates the ability to see a whole environment instead of just a single object. Intromission was furthered and developed by a medieval scholar named Ibn al-Haitham, also known as Alhazen, who wrote the *Book of Optics*. It was Alhazen who explored the anatomy of the eye. His research and scientific methods ultimately led to what science supports today: the theory of intromission. Long gone are the days of ocular beams and goddess fire igniting our pupils. Modern ophthalmology is very clear about the science of sight.

Why, then, has the Evil Eye survived so many centuries? Why is it still prevalent in so many cultures and countries? To our ancestors, the beams that were thought to have enabled sight surely had other potent properties. If a simple glance could reveal the details of objects and the environment, imagine what an *intentional* stare could accomplish. Eyes—the very process of sight, in fact—were weaponized early on in human history. This derives from the idea that the eyes are active organs, capable of accomplishing much more than sight. It is evident that the theory of extramission has never completely faded from human consciousness, but does the theory still hold validity?

When examining the Evil Eye in relation to the theory of extramission, there is a particular phenomenon that is frequently overlooked—a phenomenon that most people have experienced.

It has to do with "the sense of being stared at." Consider the following examples.

1. You are browsing leisurely through a store, wrapped up in your own thoughts, when a sudden feeling of uneasiness jolts you out of your reverie and into the awareness that you're being watched. Your head snaps up and you see that someone is, in fact, staring at you. It doesn't matter if the person is nearby or far away. It doesn't matter if the person is an old friend or a complete stranger. The truth is that you *felt* the weight of another person's stare. A hand didn't tap your shoulder, nor did a gust of wind ruffle your hair and cause you to look up. What you sensed was an energy being directed at you—an energy transmitted from someone else's eyes. How can this be explained?

2. You are standing in a crowded room when someone catches your eye. The person might be an ex-lover, a secret crush, or a friend with whom you lost touch. You don't want to talk to the person or alert them of your presence, so you stop what you're doing and just *stare* at them. You do this in a (seemingly) covert manner, hiding in a corner to avoid being seen. The person of interest is engaged in conversation with someone else, the room is loud and crowded, and there's absolutely no chance of being caught in the act of gawking . . . until the subject of your attention abruptly turns their head and *stares right back at you*. You suddenly find yourself trapped in the awkward situation you wanted to avoid. How did the person you were carefully observing sense that they were being stared at?

This phenomenon is more than coincidental. Science tells us that energy does not shoot from the eyes and "touch" the environment in our field of vision, yet most of us have felt another person's stare beaming in on us. Most of us have also experienced that shocking moment when our own stare was caught or realized by the person we were staring at. These instances lend credence to the theory that our eyes may, in fact, be capable of emitting energy. When we consider the study of quantum mechanics, energy fields, and emerging evidence that proves the interconnectedness of objects, extramission—even at a minimal level— does not seem farfetched.

There is scientific data on the topic. Rupert Sheldrake, Ph.D., an English scientist whose research includes paranormal subjects, explores this phenomenon in his book, *The Sense of Being Stared At: And Other Unexplained Powers of Human Minds* (Park Street Press, 2013). His academic paper of the same title (published by the *Journal of Consciousness* in 2005), also examines the theory in relation to the animal kingdom and predator/prey relationships.

In 2010, Dr. Colin Andrew Ross published "Hypotheses: The Electrophysiological Basis of Evil Eye Belief" in *Anthropology of Consciousness* magazine (Vol. 21, Issue 1). The paper details an experiment in which extramission was detected in an electromagnetic signal projected from an individual's eyes. Though not definitive, the experiment provides the basis for further study.

For those who believe in the Evil Eye, no scientific evidence is needed to support its existence because their lived experiences are visceral and absolute. They know that emotion—be it overt jealousy or concealed ill will—can produce tangible effects and have dangerous repercussions.

WHY THE EYE? MORE THAN A POP CULTURE TREND

There are beliefs and customs from centuries past that have no place in our modern world. Some are outlandish; many are horrifyingly archaic. To the civilizations that kept them, however, such practices were commonplace. Over time, many of these beliefs became superstitions. Some people still refuse to walk under ladders, and others knock on wood to ward away evil, but the anxiety that fuels those actions isn't necessarily woven into the fabric of their everyday lives. Even superstitions that have popular resonance—like not stepping on a crack—are largely referenced tongue-in-cheek.

Unlike most ancient superstitions, however, the Evil Eye has survived millennia. Neither the passage of time nor the demands of an increasingly secular society have mitigated its efficacy. What is its staying power?

"The belief system survives because it serves a psychological and social function," said folklorist and author Dr. Sabina Magliocco, whom I interviewed for an article I wrote about the Evil Eye that was published in 2021 by *The Wild Hunt*. "Evil Eye belief is usually about social relations, not supernatural ones. It reflects the fear of envy that characterizes small-scale societies the world over. In tightly knit, egalitarian communities with a shared concept of limited good—that is, a belief that the amount of available good things is limited—one person's good fortune necessarily comes at the expense of someone else. That applies not only to material wealth but to fertility, happiness, success, and other intangibles. Therefore, people believe that if they have something good, others will envy them."

Dr. Gideon Bohak, author of *Ancient Jewish Magic: A History* (Cambridge University Press, 2011) and professor of Jewish Philosophy and Religious Studies at Tel Aviv University, also contributed to the article and offered his view on the Eye's enduring power. "I think this is a combination of several things," he said. "On the one hand, the Evil Eye is a form of jealousy, which makes people afraid that the jealousy of others in their own success might somehow hurt them. On the other, the very gaze of people (and animals, especially dangerous animals) is psychologically very disturbing. I think this why the Eye became such a focal point of human fears of how other humans might harm them—on purpose or even inadvertently."

Magliocco also touched on a bit of psychology, noting how personal behaviors can foster belief in the Eye. "We all have people with whom we might be in conflict—neighbors, ex-spouses, coworkers," she said. "Evil Eye belief allows us to project bad feelings on to the person we are in conflict with, as well as explaining misfortune: it's *their* fault we have a headache or upset stomach because they wished us ill through the Evil Eye! *They* caused us to have a run of bad luck because they're angry with us; we can hold ourselves blameless."

The sociological and psychological aspects behind the Eye's staying power cannot be overlooked, but to those who perform old rituals rooted in cultural and family practices, the Eye is real and a force unto itself.

Dimitri, a first-generation Greek-American, was raised in a traditional Eastern Orthodox household. The Evil Eye—mati in Greek—was a part of his everyday life. He was a teenager when an aunt passed on to him their family's secret prayer to diagnose and cure the Eye.

"There's never been a time in my life when I didn't believe in it," he told me when I interviewed him in January 2022. "Growing up, I saw the Eye strike people all the time, and I also saw how they improved once it was removed. It's never left the world and it never will because people inherently believe in it, whether they admit it or not. You can *feel* a person's bad vibes through their eyes."

According to Dimitri, the ritual to diagnose and remove the Eye is the reason for its staying power. "It just works," he stated firmly. "I can't explain why, my aunt couldn't explain why, but what I know is this: when someone has the Eye taken off in the right way, they become instant believers. Their life changes almost immediately because however the Eye was hurting them—it all disappears once the Eye is removed."

Opinions about the Eye's ubiquity aren't always affirmative, especially among practitioners. Amalia, a mother of three and grandmother of nine, was born in Italy and immigrated to Canada in her early twenties. She learned how to detect and banish malocchio from her own mother. A practicing Catholic, Amalia has a decidedly ominous perspective about the Eye's growing popularity.

"Thirty years ago, I used to take off malocchio only for my family and a few close friends," she said. "Now the requests are nonstop. I always thought interest in malocchio would fade away as I got older, but the opposite has happened. Why is that? Because people are scared. Sometimes a person's bad feelings toward you can do more damage than a knife. No one's immune to the Evil Eye."

Recent statistical information may prove that very point—or, at the very least, support it. Amulets and talismans are worn by people of all faiths and ethnicities, and the fashion research platform Lyst reported a 58% increase in sales of Evil Eye jewelry in 2020. The fashion industry as a whole has responded to this fierce consumer demand. Designer Stuart Weitzman created the "eyelove" and "eyelovemore" shoe designs, emblazoned with images of the *nazar* in various colors. Coach 1941 placed a nazar pattern on sweaters, and Evil Eye–themed T-shirts by Urban Outfitters were a hit among shoppers. Other retailers have created bedspreads, linens, and doormats. In 2020, Meghan Markle, Duchess of Sussex, made headlines when she wore a series of nazar pendants. The Evil Eye trends regularly across numerous online platforms as well.

The Eye has also long had a prominent place in media. In 2020, Priyanka Chopra produced a film titled *Evil Eye*, and the Eye as a supernatural force or cultural mainstay can be found in iconic films like *My Big Fat Greek Wedding* and *Fiddler on the Roof*. The hugely popular television series *The Sopranos* referenced malocchio in several episodes. Black Sabbath, Motorhead, and Billy Idol have all recorded songs with a single title: "Evil Eye." Bob Dylan, the legendary singer/songwriter and Nobel Prize winner, mentions the Evil Eye in a few songs, perhaps most notably in "Disease of Conceit."

It isn't only in popular culture that we find the Evil Eye and practices related to it. Many rites of passage are rooted in the Eye and avoiding its wrath. This is perhaps most evident when it comes to marriage. Many brides wear a veil to conceal their eyes, thereby avoiding direct visual contact with the envious stares of others. The tradition of throwing rice at the bride and groom is believed to deflect the Evil Eye. In Ashkenazi Jewish tradition, it's not uncommon to see the bride circle the groom seven times beneath the chuppah. The movement is believed to create a kind of wall around the groom, protecting him from the admiring (or envious) glances of other women.

Think about everyday life. Some of our most common sayings and idioms refer directly to the power of our eyes. Have you ever instructed someone to "look me in the eye" when trying to gauge whether or not they're telling the truth? Has anyone ever told you that you "have eyes in the back of your head?" We've all "turned a blind eye" to a person or situation we've wanted to forget or ignore. Trying to conceal your feelings about a person or situation might be met with the expression "The eyes don't lie."

THE EYE: A GLOBAL GLIMPSE

To many, the Evil Eye is a simple (and singular) concept. In truth, however, customs and cures differ from country to country or particular regions of the world. While it's impossible to capture the breadth and scope of the Eye completely, this section is a brief sojourn through several countries and their Evil Eye practices.

Belief in the Evil Eye is widespread in Africa. While envy and ill will comprise the crux of the Eye's power, other factors like malefic spirits and witchcraft also play a significant role in its manifestation. In Ethiopia (most notably the highlands), the Eye is known as *buda*, which refers to both the curse itself and the people believed to possess the ability to cast it. Buda is blamed for numerous misfortunes: illness, infertility, ailing livestock, blighted crops. Even minor accidents are attributed to this malevolent force. It is believed that a person who holds the power to cast buda can shapeshift into a hyena, thereby granting the caster anonymity. But when it comes to the Evil Eye, not everyone is regarded as a threat. Buda is primarily associated with ironworkers, craftspeople, weavers, and other artisans, as well as the Beta Israel, or Ethiopian Jews—generally those who occupy a low rung on the socioeconomic ladder. The theory here isn't unique: people who have very little are envious of those who have a lot. The poor and marginalized do not own land, and therefore covet their wealthy neighbors; in doing so, buda is unleashed.

There are several different ways to ward away buda. Ethiopian Christians often wear or carry a *kitab*, an amulet that holds tiny scrolls on which scriptural passages are inscribed. Other defensive measures include branding, shaving children's heads (lice is believed to be caused by buda), and covering the nose and mouth while outdoors. When buda strikes, the afflicted may call in a *debtera*, a layperson trained in the ways of protective rituals and magic. If a case of buda is particularly acute, an Ethiopian Orthodox priest may step in to perform an exorcism, as demonic possession is sometimes linked to the Evil Eye.

In Morocco, belief in the Eye (*al-ayn*) is widespread. Deeply rooted in both popular and Islamic culture, the Eye is primarily thought to be the result of envy, but magic and the invocation of *djinn*—an indigenous spirit that can be benevolent or meddlesome—are also common culprits. Al-ayn can afflict an individual's life in numerous ways; work, home life, health, and family matters are all fair game.

A Moroccan-American colleague once relayed to me the story of her wedding day, in which the Evil Eye played a central role. That morning, her father tripped outside of their home and injured his foot. Soon after, my colleague dropped a glass in her bedroom, which shattered into pieces. Then she learned that two family members were experiencing car trouble and would arrive late to the ceremony. Though ultimately minor hiccups, al-ayn was immediately branded the culprit. The Eye had "hit" its target. Later, as my colleague was putting on her wedding dress, she found two hamsas and several small blue beads sewn into the dress's lining. Her uncle arrived, and he ritually "cleansed" her by burning sandalwood incense and wafting it around her head, hands, and feet. From that point on, her wedding day proceeded smoothly.

The use of amulets to ward away the Eye and the performing of other rituals and spells to cure it are commonplace in Moroccan culture. Some are quick and easy, like holding up a hand after perceiving a threat or hollow compliment; known as "Five in Your Eye!" this simple gesture has mighty effects. Other magical practices utilize herbs, plants, fragrant smoke, and the recitation of Quranic verses. Another old custom in Morocco (and throughout North Africa) is the use of the henna plant; when its leaves are ground into a powder and mixed with water, a paste forms and is then used to draw tattoos, many of them talismanic and intricately beautiful. Henna is especially popular among brides in Morocco. Al-ayn is a pervasive and immensely powerful energy— so powerful that some Moroccans believe it "tracks" them like an invisible serpent.

In Sudan, it is considered inappropriate to compliment a person repeatedly because doing so can tempt the Eye to strike. Certain medical conditions, thought to be the result of jealousy or ill will, are treated through rituals and the use of incense. Libya is home to Leptis Magna, one of the best-preserved archeological sites in the world. Founded by the Phoenicians, the ancient city eventually became part of the Roman Empire and today its ruins include numerous apotropaic symbols. Among these are the winged phallus and other phallic-shaped markings, which are amuletic against the Evil Eye.

The Evil Eye is also widespread throughout Asia. In India, it has several names: *kudrishti, nazar dosh, nazar lagna, drishti, buri nazar,* and sometimes just nazar. Both a cultural and spiritual belief, nazar is rooted in the fear of envy and the damage it can do. Eyes, according to a Hindu belief, emanate powerful energy—perhaps the most powerful energy in the human body. People in India protect themselves from nazar through amulets, talismans, and practices aimed at deflecting and removing it. A common—and commonly visible—way is through the use of a *tilak,* a mark that is usually made on the forehead or cheek of infants, children, and adults; this can be done through a dab of coal or the use of *kajal,* a black pencil.

Kajal is also used to darken a woman's eyes. The theory here is one of diversion: as nazar prepares to strike, it gets distracted by the tilak and fails to hit its target. The bead is also an aversion technique. Beads are both worn and hung in homes in India; they are created with different colors, each color having a specific defensive role in warding away nazar. Other practices thought to deflect nazar include giving away one's clothing to the poor and offering prayers to the *yantra*, a mystical geometrical diagram. The yantra can also be worn as an amulet.

In India, homes are considered a prime target for the Evil Eye. In addition to hanging beads, people display sharp objects (like broken seashells) and mount mirrors directly opposite the front door to combat envious stares. Lemons and chili peppers are bound together with string and hung over doorways. After a new home is purchased, its owners may mark a white pumpkin with a dot and hang it close to the front door. If nazar is present, numerous practices are employed to remove it. For example, a woman may mix cooked rice with turmeric powder to create a ball that she will rotate around the afflicted individual's head in a counterclockwise motion; the ball is then discarded in a fire or somewhere outside of the home. Incense is a staple of nearly every home, and various types of herbal mixtures are burned to chase away nazar. Hindus may also recite mantras to deities like Bhairava, Krishna, and Shiva to cast out the negative energy.

One cannot look at a blue bead or hamsa without thinking about Turkey. Here, the Evil Eye is called *nazar boncugu*. As in Morocco and India, the Eye is a dominant belief in Turkey. The word "nazar" is often used interchangeably, referring to the Evil Eye itself and the amulet that wards it away. The ubiquitous glass blue-and-white bead can be spotted just about everywhere in Turkey—nailed to doorways, painted on walls, strung from car mirrors and the entrances to businesses. A bead that breaks, either while being worn or displayed, is believed to have "taken the hit," absorbing the curse that would have otherwise impacted a person, home, or shop. This theory is common in several countries and cultures, but in Turkey, it also extends to broken mirrors; if a mirrors cracks, nazar was at work but missed its intended target.

It is said that anyone who visits Turkey will immediately understand the nazar as a means of protection, not a charm to bring good luck or positive energy. The beads are present at all life-affirming events—births, marriages, parties and celebrations of all kinds—thereby ensuring safety from jealous onlookers. In addition to the blue-and-white bead, there is also the *muska*, this amulet is usually triangular and holds a piece of paper inscribed with scriptural passages or the name of Allah. As Turkey is a predominantly Muslim country, nazar is also deflected and cured through the recitation of a *ruqyah*—a verse or prayer from the Quran. Totems and other amulets made from the wood of the terebinth tree are believed to keep one safe from nazar because of the wood's ability to withstand harsh conditions.

In the region of Cappadocia, Turkey, "evil eye trees" are a common sight, their branches glimmering with shiny blue beads. In more rural areas, people etch protective designs onto eggshells to keep nazar away. Turkey's famous kilim rugs are frequently woven with protective symbols: the eye, the hamsa (more commonly known in Turkey as the *Fatma Ana Eli*, referring to the Hand of Fatima), and sometimes the cross, which is believed to obliterate the Evil Eye by splitting it into four parts.

Certain protective devices serve as a bridge between cultures. The Assyrian Evil Eye amulet—a piece of turquoise or a bead with two holes that represent eyes—is a prime example. What was once Assyria (the kingdom of northern Mesopotamia), is now located in southeastern Turkey and northern Iraq, and similar amulets and beliefs about the Evil Eye can be found in these territories today.

Egypt has a long and storied history when it comes to the Evil Eye, and many of the beliefs that were practiced 5,000 years ago remain prevalent. *Aien al-hasoud*—which refers to the "eye of jealousy or evil"—is feared among Egyptians, and numerous magical methods are employed to combat it. Amulets are a common sight in homes, businesses, shops, and on vehicles. Handprints, hamsas, and the Eye of Horus—known also as *wedjat* or *udjat*—are among the most frequently used. An Egyptian man I interviewed explained that speech is also an important method when it comes to combating the Evil Eye in Egypt. If someone complimented him by saying, "You're successful and always look so fit," his response would be, "Thank you, but this morning I tripped and almost broke my leg. I'm actually in a lot of pain right now." The fact that he hadn't tripped that morning (and thus wasn't experiencing any pain) is irrelevant. What matters is the strategy—by minimizing the compliment, he minimized the potential envy brewing inside of the person who offered the compliment.

Similar customs related to speech and mitigating envy exist elsewhere in the Middle East. In most Arab nations, any compliment should be immediately followed by the words *"Masha'Alla,"* which means "what God wants" or "may it be what God wants." Another custom that crosses several cultures is spitting—not for the sake of hacking up phlegm, but as a kind of on-the-spot ritual. Saliva is believed to hold tremendous power when it comes to smiting the Eye (page 57).

Both spitting and the use of particular words are common among Israelis. The simple question, "How have you been?" is often answered with *"Baruch Hashem,"* which means "Praise God." In Hebrew, the Evil Eye is called *ayin hara*, and to chase it away Israelis say *"Bli ayin hara,"* (without the evil eye). There are also other numerous ways to ward away and cure it. In markets throughout the country, one can easily find tea and spice stalls that sell mixtures of *za'atar* (a spice blend of sesame seeds, oregano, dill, thyme, and kosher salt) and sumac; the mixture is used as an incense to chase away negative energies, especially envy. The red string visible on the wrists of many Israelis is also used as an amulet.

Palestinians have traditionally used embroidery to deflect the Eye, weaving various amulets into blankets and garments. Certain amulets are crafted by inscribing prayers onto paper, after which the paper is deposited into a triangular case. Beads and stones, usually carved into the shapes of eyes, are a popular method for warding away the Eye. Specially prepared paper amulets are believed to keep the sting of jealous eyes away from homes.

Europe is home to a host of Evil Eye beliefs and traditions. The Eye in Italy (malocchio) and Greece (mati) are well-known in popular culture, but the fear of an envious stare is also prominent in Romania (where it's called *deochi*), Hungary, Poland, and Moldova; sudden illnesses like lethargy, interrupted sleep, loss of hunger, and digestive pains are believed to be signs of the Eye at work. In Malta, it's common to see an eye symbol painted onto the sides of boats. In Scotland, the Evil Eye (*droch-shuil*) is treated by tying and knotting a length of string around an afflicted object. Allowing the string to disintegrate will wither the curse's power.

The Evil Eye also has a prominent place in Slavic culture. The home is considered a prime target for jealous or ill-intended stares, and to deflect them, ornately carved platbands (a flat arch or a group of moldings) are placed around windows and doors, and sometimes along railings and rooftops. Children are believed to be especially vulnerable to the dangers of envy. To deflect the Eye, a child is given a handmade doll that also serves as a guardian against evil spirits; garbed in beautiful attire, the doll is usually faceless, as it's believed that bad energy can enter a doll via its facial features. Another way to combat the Evil Eye in Slavic culture is through embroidery. Various patterns are woven into clothing, blankets, and curtains as a kind of apotropaic magic.

Among the best cures for Evil Eye sickness are running water and salt.

The West Indies and the Caribbean are home to a vast array of Evil Eye beliefs. Called *maljo* in Trinidad and Tobago and *mal de ojo* in Cuba and the Dominican Republic, the Eye is believed to be a source of illness, financial woes, and bad luck. One of the most common ways to deflect the Eye is through the use of the color blue. Hung on fences that surround homes are blue bottles, ornaments, and sometimes blue marks made with paint. I interviewed a woman from Trinidad who carried a bright blue handkerchief in her purse; if she ever felt an envious glare aimed at her, she reached for the handkerchief and "blotted" the air in front of her. Jumbie beads—red-and-black colored seeds of the rosary pea plant—are strung together and worn as a bracelet to chase away the Evil Eye. Other methods include the use of jet beads, making a protective device by tying together peacock feathers and palm leaves, and creating a satchel filled with the skins of onion and garlic, pepper, and a lock of hair. Powdered orris root, also carried in a satchel, is believed to keep a romantic relationship safe from the Evil Eye.

In South America, Central America, Mexico, and among Latino immigrants in the United States, belief in mal de ojo is immensely strong. Initially believed to have been brought over by colonizers, many now theorize that mal de ojo is a combination of European customs and indigenous folk practices. Those practices are alive and well today. To rid a child of mal de ojo, for example, a piece of yarn or string is rubbed around the child's eyes. The ringing of bells is also a common cure, as the noise either distracts or disperses negative energy. One of the best-known remedies against mal de ojo involves an egg. After rubbing an egg over an afflicted person's body, the egg is deposited in a glass of water and placed under the bed; in some instances, the egg is cracked into the water and the yolk interpreted.

The Evil Eye is the most feared curse in world. Oceans separate countries, countries have different cultures, cultures have different languages, and languages have different dialects. But threaded through these differences is the ubiquitous and ever-present belief that a single, silent glance can unleash destruction.

CHAPTER TWO

HISTORY, ORIGINS, AND TRADITIONS

In 2021, the Israel Antiquities Authority unveiled to the world a 1,500-year-old amulet believed to have been used to protect women and children from the Evil Eye. Originally discovered by a resident of the village of Arbel in the Galilee, the amulet bears a series of elaborate images and inscriptions. On one side is an eye pierced by four arrows and accompanied by a scorpion, a snake, a bird, and lions. On the flip side is what appears to be a haloed male figure on a horse, thrusting a sphere at a female figure lying on the ground. The image is encircled by Greek lettering that reads: "The One God who Conquers Evil."

Shortly after the amulet was unveiled to the public, Dr. Eitan Klein, deputy director of the Antiquities Theft Prevention Unit, made a statement via a press release. "The amulet is part of a group of fifth-sixth-century CE amulets from the Levant that were prob-ably produced in the Galilee and Lebanon," he explained. "This group of amulets is sometimes called 'Solomon's Seal,' and the rider is depicted overcoming the evil spirit—in this case, a female identified with the mythological figure Gello/Gyllou, who threatens women and children and is associated with the evil eye."

An astonishing discovery, the amulet itself is one of countless archaeological finds that prove the ancient origins of the Evil Eye. How old are those origins? When did the concept of the Evil Eye take root in human consciousness? There have always been, currently are, and probably always will be, different answers to these questions. Many scholars and historians theorize that the Evil Eye belief complex goes back at least 5,000 years. Others have cited 10,000-year-old drawings discovered on cave walls in Spain that resemble warding symbols. Whichever way you look at it, the history of the Eye encompasses a wide swath of time.

It's important to note that there is a difference between the Evil Eye as a concept and the apotropaic devices that have been unearthed all over the world. In *The Evil Eye: A Classic Account of an Ancient Superstition*, Frederick Thomas Elworthy explored the phenomenon in great depth and proposed a compelling theory: "The origin of the belief is lost in the obscurity of prehistoric ages. The enlightened call it superstition, but it holds sway over the people of many countries, savage as well as civilized, and must be set down as one of the hereditary and instinctive convictions of mankind."

While there is no definitive way to pinpoint when or where the idea of the Evil Eye curse began, antiquity has given us a great deal of evidence about how strongly ancient civilizations believed in it. What may be the oldest piece of evidence of Evil Eye belief and practices to deflect it are Sumerian incantations in cuneiform texts, which date back to the third millennium BCE.

This makes sense when we consider that the Sumerians and Akkadians believed in a host of supernatural forces and entities. As in most of the ancient world, they practiced divination, recited prayers and incantations, and looked to "the other world" for clues about the world in which they lived. From their inscriptions on clay tablets, it's evident that they feared evil spirits and evil in general and used amulets to ward away or counteract such attacks.

But it is the incantations referencing the Evil Eye that provide convincing evidence. One such incantation from the Old Babylonian Period, (included in John H. Elliott's *Beware the Evil Eye: The Evil Eye in the Bible and the Ancient World*), gives insight into the wide range of complexities and damages caused by the Eye. The Eye is described as the source of numerous misfortunes impacting crops, cattle, and humans. Also mentioned are animals, a young man, a young woman, a nurse and baby. Certain incantations describe the Eye as a nebulous entity that is both "restless" and "roaming." In others, the Eye is the result of a person who possesses the ability to cast it. In another example from Elliott's book, an Akkadian text details a witch as the culprit of several catastrophes, including stealing a man's virility and a young woman's beauty.

Though scholars have challenged the theory that belief in the Evil Eye was widespread in Mesopotamia, the incantations seem to prove that it was. Nearly every aspect of life is mentioned or alluded to, from food and crops to pregnancy, virility, children, and overall health. Indeed, the Eye held the power of life and death. The incantations also illustrate the Eye as having much more than human qualities; it was described as a dragon, associated with various demons, and in full possession of horrifying powers.

Amulets also highlight the Evil Eye's prevalence in Mesopotamia, with the earliest ones dating back to 3,300 BC. These amulets, resembling abstract idols with incised eyes, were excavated in Tell Brak, one of the most ancient cities of Mesopotamia (modern day Syria). These objects were discovered in a building in Tell Brak that is today known as the Eye Temple. The "idols" likely suggest that the eye was perceived as an organ, an image, and an object of great power among Sumerian, Babylonian, and Assyrian people.

The belief that the eye possessed extraordinary properties is also evident in ancient Egypt, where one of the civilization's most iconic images was (and remains) the Eye of Horus. Also known as the wedjat or udjat, the Eye of Horus was a powerful symbol of protection; it was used as a funerary symbol, painted on coffins and buried with pharaohs so that the dead could "see" as they made their journey to the next realm. Other theories claim that the Eye of Horus may have represented the moon in its waning and waxing phases. A fixture of meaning and magic, it was carved on stones and boats and rendered on hieroglyphs. As a talisman, the Eye of Horus represents healing and rebirth.

As early as the 6th century BCE in Greece, images of eyes appeared on Chalcidian drinking vessels, and these "eye-cups" were used for protection. Ancient Greeks certainly feared the gaze of another person, but scholars have noted that they may also have feared malevolent spirits entering their bodies when they opened their mouths to drink. As in ancient Egypt, eyes were painted on boats that traversed the Aegean Sea. All are examples of apotropaic magic—the use of symbols to deflect misfortune.

In ancient Rome, the *oculus malus* (Evil Eye) was blamed for any number of ailments and misfortunes, but the phallus became the primary amulet to ward it away. It was familiar, a reminder of power, virility, and fertility. Phallic imagery was evident on wall and floor mosaics and even carved onto the sides of buildings.

Interestingly, the Romans believed that the Eye could be overcome or, at the very least, weakened. Numerous mosaics and carvings depict the Eye being assailed by various objects or symbols. The most well-known example of such an image is the mosaic from the House of the Evil Eye at Antioch (now modern-day Turkey), in which an eye—the Evil Eye, no doubt—is encircled by a snake, a dog, a leopard, a raven, and a scorpion, as well as a sword. A similar image from the archaeological site of Leptis Magna is perhaps even more striking, as it depicts a two-legged beast ejaculating into an Evil Eye.

Some of the most convincing evidence of the Evil Eye's prominence in the Greco-Roman era can be found in its literature. Here are some examples:

"No notice is taken of a little evil, but when it increases it strikes the eye."

—Aristotle

"My friend," said Socrates, "do not be boastful, lest some evil eye put to rout the argument that is to come. That, however, is in the hands of God. Let us, in Homeric fashion, change the foe and test the worth of what you say."

—Plato, *Phaedo*

"It was not his duty to look with an evil eye upon a man who had made it his business to support or propose measures worthy of our traditions, and was resolved to stand by such measures: nor to treasure vindictively the memory of private annoyances. Nor was it his duty to hold his peace dishonestly and deceptively, as you so often do."

—Demosthenes, *On the Crown*

The precise origins of the Evil Eye will never be known, but archeology, Egyptology, and studies about ancient cultures and magic have demonstrated that the Eye is much more than a superstition. To fully understand the Evil Eye's power as a cultural and sociological phenomenon, however, we must look away from the past and into its presence today.

THE EVIL EYE IN RELIGIOUS, ETHNIC, AND CULTURAL TRADITIONS

Folk magic can be defined in many ways, but it is essentially the magic practiced by common folk. We have all heard stories about the village witch, the shaman, the soothsayer, the wise elderly man or woman who could cure illness by walking into the forest to gather specific herbs. Sometimes herbs weren't even needed. An old incantation and the gentle cadence of its words did the trick. These practices and beliefs differ greatly among cultures and geographic locations, but what folk magic practitioners generally share is a connection to—and reliance on—their own environments, be they wooded or urban.

In our fast-paced technological world, it's hard to imagine such a thing. Society has been programmed to label the old ways of our ancestors "primitive" and "backward." And the notion of magic? Many still equate magic with Disney cartoons, unicorns, and the fantastical stories that dominate our bookshelves and television screens. Because of that, too many have lost what they need most—a connection to nature.

Nature is within you and around you. If you look up from this page and see brick walls and steel beams and all the other trappings of the concrete jungle, remember this: nature is in the bowl of water you can place on your kitchen counter; it's crackling in the flame of a candle or match. Reciting a prayer or incantation is nature because your breath is air. That little patch of grass sprouting up through the broken concrete where you parked your car or stepped off the bus? That's nature.

Folk magic is about recognizing the resources in your natural environment and then making magic out of those resources. When our ancestors were faced with the threat of the Evil Eye, they didn't have the ability to log on to the internet and Google a remedy. The rituals, spells, and prayers they used to diagnose and cure misfortune and ill health were born out of necessity and a belief that the mundane and the miraculous could intersect.

Sounds like good old witchcraft, right? Today, not all folk magic practitioners identify as witches, sorcerers, or healers. Sometimes they don't even identify with anything that waxes particularly mystical. My maternal grandparents practiced Italian folk magic but would never have considered themselves witches. They were Roman Catholics who incorporated a kind of vernacular magic into their everyday lives. This is true of most folk magic traditions. The old rituals and incantations that likely had pre-Christian roots were syncretized with Christianity long ago.

Folk magic is about practice, not religion as we see it. The former is practical, functional, and concerned with everyday life. The latter can be about structure, organized systems, moral codes, and clearing a path to the afterlife.

This is precisely why folk magic has survived. Culture, heritage, and indigenous traditions all factor into folk magic. But if there's one common thread that winds through every folk magic tradition—be it Italian, Greek, Latinx, Jewish, or Afro-Caribbean—it's the Evil Eye. Across cultures and continents, its rituals are still practiced—different but similar, simple but multi-layered, ordinary but utterly transformative.

Christianity and the Evil Eye

Superstition and religion rarely go hand-in-hand. The sacred texts many of us were instructed to learn, live by, and extol often reveal teachings that are opposed to the cultural beliefs with which we were raised. This has certainly been my own personal experience. In my earliest memories, I can still see my maternal grandmother standing over a bowl of water, her left hand holding a spoon filled with olive oil and her right hand making the sign of the cross. I can also see my maternal grandfather standing in an overgrown garden, looking up at the dusky sky to make sure the moon's phase was complimenting his patch of tomatoes. How about that time a poor unknowing soul (a non-Italian) tried to step over a toddler who was quietly playing with her doll on the living room floor? I can still hear the shrill screams that erupted from the kitchen as my great aunts and uncles rushed to intercept the grievous error. (In many parts of southern and central Italy, it is still believed that stepping over a child will stunt their growth and cause a host of other problems.) Hundreds of superstitions shaped my formative years, but these curious beliefs were rooted in Italian culture and not, I eventually learned, religion.

Catholic school was a profound—and, at times, profoundly confusing—experience. Most of the nuns who educated me were adamant that I *not* extend my index and pinkie fingers to defend myself from bad comments. When I was in the fifth grade, one of them—let's call her Sister Tiffany—spotted the red *cornetto* (a small horn-shaped amulet popular among Italians) hanging from a chain around my neck; the chain also held a medal of Saint Anthony of Padua, but Sister Tiffany flew into a red-cheeked rage and ordered me to take the amulet off. I did as I was told to do. At home that night, however, I was instructed to put the corno back on. I was also told to be more circumspect about the T-shirts I chose to wear on the rare occasions when students were allowed to go to school out of uniform (an open or thin collar revealed the amulet).

None of it made sense. Nearly all of the Italian-American kids in my neighborhood wore a little red horn around their necks. Why was it permissible (and encouraged) to wear amulets and regard superstitions everywhere *except* in church and at school?

A couple of years later, Father Dolan patiently explained to me that I should not put my faith in *things*. Only God had the power to protect me from harm. Things like amulets and old incantations were just plain silly. There was, of course, more leeway when it came to wearing a saint medal; this was okay so long as I understood that not even the saints could fully protect me in a moment of peril. The saints could tap Jesus on the shoulder and get his attention, but they couldn't prevent what God willed. So as for that pesky Evil Eye... well, Father Dolan told me not to think about it because it wasn't real.

This is how I learned early on that being Italian and being Catholic were often different experiences. The same was true for my classmates who came from similarly ethnic families. We had been raised to abide by numerous superstitions—especially the Evil Eye—but the Roman Catholic Church was very clear when it came to such matters: anything that opposed or detracted from the rigid edicts set forth by the Vatican was wrong.

That's still true today. It's also true of other Christian denominations and their respective authorities. The Eastern Orthodox Church, for example, does not support belief in the Evil Eye, but mati is an inexorable part and practice of Greek culture, not to mention Middle Eastern and Slavic cultures.

The Evil Eye is prevalent in Christianity today because of spiritual syncretism. The belief that envy can curse a person or object was firmly established long before the advent of Christianity, and as people assimilated to conversion—forced or otherwise—they retained practices native to their homelands, cultures, local villages, and families. Diagnosing and curing the Evil Eye is an example of this. Today, many Christians label the Eye an "occult concept," claiming that it has nothing to do with Christianity; some have even branded it downright heretical. Interestingly, however, the Bible tells a different story. Jesus of Nazareth believed in the destructive powers of the Evil Eye and mentioned it in his "Sermon on the Mount":

"The eye is the lamp of the body. If your eyes are healthy, your whole body will be full of light. But if your eyes are unhealthy, your whole body will be full of darkness. If then the light within you is darkness, how great is that darkness!"

This is clearly a reference to envy, greed, and ill will. When we covet others and what they have, we do damage to ourselves. When we see what we *don't* have and become angry or resentful about it—especially while staring at a person who just might be enjoying what's missing from our own lives—we restrict our ability to recognize and be grateful for the blessings that exist in the present moment.

This passage also makes us wonder if perhaps Jesus of Nazareth was lending credence to the theory of extramission. If the eyes are "the lamps of the body," what power is fueling the lamps? Emotion. Like electricity, human emotion can create beauty, harmony, and stability; conversely, emotions can create chaos, danger, and death. In the "Sermon on the Mount," Jesus of Nazareth is telling us that our emotions are potent energy—a force emitted not only through the process of sight, but also in how we actively choose to look at and interact with the world.

This brings us to the "Parable of the Workers in the Vineyard." (Matthew 20: 1–16) Here, a group of workers let known their dismay at being paid the same amount as their fellow laborers, who didn't clock in as many hours. Why should those who worked less get more than they deserve? (A very universal question.) The landowner offers a thoughtful response: "Is it not lawful for me to do what I will with mine own? Is thine eye evil, because I am good?" This is another reference to envy and its damaging power. The first group of workers is actually doubly jealous—not only of their fellow laborers, but also of the man who has enough money to do with it exactly what he wishes to do.

Examining this parable is difficult. In considering the socio-economic injustices of society today, many may feel a kind of kinship with the disgruntled laborers and their envy. If you worked a ten-hour day and got paid the same amount as the person who worked two hours, would you feel, as most of us have felt, tremendous injustice?

In his letter to the Galatians, Paul the Apostle (also called the Epistle of Saint Paul the Apostle to the Galatians), addresses his converts with the following words: "O you uncomprehending Galatians, who has injured you with an Evil Eye?' (Galatians 3:1)." In certain biblical translations, the Evil Eye is replaced with the word *bewitched*.

In *Beware the Evil Eye, Volume 1: The Evil Eye in the Bible and the Ancient World*, scholar John Elliott theorizes that the scriptures, in their original languages, hold as many as twenty-four references to the Evil Eye, and that most of those references have been veiled by modern biblical translations.

Hinduism and the Evil Eye

Believed by some scholars and theologians to be the world's oldest religion, a number of Hindu customs date back more than 4,000 years. Hindu practice comprises several philosophies and traditions; as such, it embraces a variety of religious and spiritual ideologies and is sometimes considered a "way of life" for adherents, but all Hindus share a belief in dharma—a tenet of living that emphasizes good conduct and morality.

Many forms of Hinduism worship a single deity—the Brahman—while still recognizing other gods and goddesses. There are believed to be more than one billion Hindu practitioners worldwide today, with as many as 95% of those residing in India. The primary sacred texts of Hinduism are the Rig Veda, the Samaveda, Yajurveda, and Atharvaveda. Other spiritually significant texts include the Upanishads, the Bhagavad Gita, 18 Puranas, Ramayana, and Mahabharata.

In the Hindu faith, the Evil Eye is known as kudrishti and buri nazar. Here, the Eye is rooted in envy, jealousy, and general ill will. Belief in kudrishti is widespread among Hindus. The prevalence of kudrishti is particularly interesting from a theological perspective, as Hindus believe in the concept of karma, a universal law that determines an individual's experience of life based on past good or bad deeds. Countless Hindus, however, blame illness or misfortune not on their own karma but on kudrishti—the Evil Eye. Numerous practices are believed to both deflect and cure kudrishti. In addition to chanting mantras and making offerings to deities, many Hindus may hang in their homes an image of a fearsome demon in hopes that it will scare away the Eye. When it comes to protection, among the most popular Hindu deities are Vishnu (protector of the universe), Ganesha (remover of obstacles), and Shiva (the destroyer). Prayers and rituals differ among Hindus, as some communities embrace particular deities that other communities do not.

Folk practices are common among Hindus, especially where the Evil Eye is concerned. To ward it away, a Hindu might wear a *nazar* or a yantra. To break the curse of the Eye, another Hindu might smash a coconut in front of a statue of Ganesha.

Islam and the Evil Eye

The *Encyclopaedia of Islam* is very clear about the Evil Eye, defining it as the cause of numerous physical ailments and medical conditions, from pain and fever to sexual dysfunction and sterility. Other symptoms are rapid weight loss, headaches, lethargy, and anxiety. According to the *Encyclopaedia*, an envious or malignant stare can lead to death: "It is believed that the evil eye may have fatal consequences and a *hadith* even specifies it as the cause of half of all human deaths (a Moroccan proverb puts the figure at two-thirds.)"

As with other faiths that acknowledge the Evil Eye, Islam views the curse as all-encompassing, capable of harming animals, homes, vehicles, and appliances. When it comes to the Quran itself, scholars generally reference verses 51 and 52 of chapter 68, al-Qalam, as being linked to the Evil Eye: "And indeed, those who disbelieve would almost make you slip with their eyes when they hear the message, and they say: 'Indeed, he is mad. But it is not except a reminder to the worlds.'"

According to *hadith*—the collected traditions of the Prophet Muhammad—the Prophet said: "The evil eye is real. If anything were to overtake the divine decree, it would be the evil eye." Muslims employ numerous practices to combat it; these practices include performing ruqyah—the recitation of specific verses—and rituals rooted in folk magic. Many Muslims believe that the Prophet even prescribed a cure for the Eye, instructing the afflicted to "perform ablutions" (baths) to dispel its harmful effects.

Early in the writing of this book, I interviewed a Muslim man who admitted that he thought about the Evil Eye every day and often attributed minor obstacles to its power. A week earlier, for example, he got a flat tire on his way home from work; while changing it on the side of the highway, he made a mental list of the people who might have been responsible for cursing him. He finally nailed down the culprits, recalling how he had walked into a colleague's office, where he found two of his coworkers gossiping. They stared at him before going off to their own posts; those stares, he said, had been laced with jealousy.

The man had recently been promoted. Fearing the Evil Eye, he had tried to persuade his supervisor to refrain from announcing the promotion, but the announcement went out via email nonetheless; this, the man believed, had turned him into "a walking target." In the end, it wasn't that big of a deal: he vanquished the dangerous energy through daily prayer, and as a Muslim, he accepted the Eye's existence completely and took necessary precautions to battle it. He kept an amulet in his pocket and had several in his home.

The use of amulets and talismans against the Evil Eye is common in Muslim culture, despite the prohibition against such practices in Islam. In 2021, the state-run religious authority in Turkey, the Diyanet, published a *fatwa*—a legal decree made by a religious authority—to that effect: "Although the nature and condition of the evil eye are not known precisely, it is accepted by religion that some people can create negative effects with their gaze. In our religion, attitudes, behaviors, and beliefs that attribute the ultimate influence on anything other than Allah are forbidden. For this reason, it is not permissible to wear evil eye amulets and similar things around the neck or anywhere for the purpose of benefiting from them."

The announcement reportedly surprised Muslims in Turkey, where the use of amulets to ward away the Eye is virtually ubiquitous. But the fatwa appears to have had little (if any) impact on the use of amulets—their popularity remains solid.

In addition to saying "ma sha'allah" when giving a compliment, many Muslims recite what are known as the "Evil Eye" verses, and even wear these verses as amulets. Another protective practice is the hanging of frames or parchments inscribed with the four short chapters in the Qur'an that begin with "Qul."

Judaism and the Evil Eye

During morning prayers, many practicing Jewish people recite a set of blessings called the *Birkhot Ha-Shahar*, which asks God to protect them from all kinds of evil. Parts of the prayer are as follows: *May we find grace, love, and compassion in your sight and in the sight of all who look upon us this day and every day.* This is followed later with: *May it be Your will, Adonai, my God and God of my ancestors, to protect me this day, and every day, from insolence in others and from arrogance in myself. Save me from vicious people, from evil neighbors, and from corrupt companions. Preserve me from misfortune and from powers of destruction. Save me from harsh judgments, spare me from ruthless opponents, be they members of the covenant or not.*

The Evil Eye is very much implied here. The mention of the sight or gaze of others has the strongest tie-in to the Eye. And, of course, envy is a part of what fuels vicious people. A harsh judgment can arise from jealousy, and ruthless opponents often become ruthless because they see it as their only choice when coveting the attributes of another.

Though not explicitly mentioned in the Torah, the Evil Eye is deeply implied in certain moments. In Genesis (49:22), for example, the dying patriarch Jacob blesses his son Joseph, saying he will be like a fruitful vine by a fountain, hanging over a wall. The rabbis of the Talmud (Bava Batra 118b) change the reading of a Hebrew word from the passage to reinterpret the blessing to mean that Joseph's descendants will never be susceptible to the Evil Eye. That blessing—reduced over time to the phrase *ben porat yosef* (translated, it means *a fruitful son*), which comprise the first three words of the blessing—is now used by Sephardi Jews to ward off the Evil Eye, envy, and jealousy.

In another moment, the rabbis say that the Eye played a role in the story of Hagar and Sarah, the mothers of Ishmael and Isaac, Abraham's sons. They claim (Bereshit Rabbah 45) that Hagar had a miscarriage before she was pregnant with Ishmael and that she lost the first baby as result of the evil glance cast by Sarah.

The Rosh Hashanah ritual of Tashlich—when Jews cast pieces of bread into the water to symbolize their casting off of sins—is done at a body of water because it is believed that fish cannot be harmed by the Evil Eye.

From the Talmudic text Bava Batra (2b:9) comes the following advice: "It is prohibited for a person to stand in another's field and look at his crop while the grain is standing, because he casts an evil eye upon it and thereby causes him damage, and the same is true for a garden."

According to Rebbe Nachman of Breslov, the legendary Hasidic teacher, the Evil Eye should never be dismissed as mere superstition. "Take care, there is much power in a glance. If accompanied by a malicious thought, it can cause harm. This is what is known as the evil eye. Have a good eye. Always see good in others. Spiritual awareness depends on it. Spiritual awareness is lost when people dull their hearts with jealousy and develop an evil eye." (#27, *Likkutei Moran* [1–54])

In rabbinic literature, there is also the strong notion about *yetzer hara*—the inclination to do evil. In certain teachings, the yetzer hara is paired with the Evil Eye, and here arises the matter of the "evil inclination," or the emotions we harbor internally. One's gaze is a representation of the thoughts and feelings that fester within us. If our internal dialogue is filled with envy and greed, those very emotions can manifest through a glance or gaze.

In the books of Exodus (20: 2–17) and Deuteronomy (5: 6–21) appear the Ten Commandments, the laws God gave to Moses on Mount Sinai. It is believed by many scholars, rabbis, and theologians that the 10th Commandment—*You shall not covet*—is a direct reference to the Evil Eye.

Mal de Ojo: The Evil Eye in Latin America

Belief in the Evil Eye is widespread in Latin America. The most common theory among scholars is that mal de ojo was brought over by the Spanish with their colonization, but many practitioners believe it existed as a part of indigenous practices and traditions.

Mateo, an educator who currently resides in the Midwest, is one of four children born to immigrant parents. Raised in two cultures, he was drawn early on to the mystical aspects of his Mexican heritage, which included Catholicism and numerous folk practices. By the time he was a teenager, however, Mateo had begun drifting away from his interest in all things mystical. He went away to college, majored in the physical sciences, and commenced his teaching career immediately after earning his degree. As the years passed, he grew more detached from the aspects of his culture that had once brought him joy. He rarely went to his native Texas and struggled to maintain healthy relationships with his family members. Then, shortly after his thirty-eighth birthday, he got sick.

Mateo spent two days in the hospital, and was stunned when all of his medical tests came back normal. No scientific reason for his illness could be diagnosed.

"The doctors told me it was stress, but I couldn't believe that," Mateo admitted. In desperation to discover the root of his health problems, he caved in to his mother's suggestion that he return home to Texas. Once there, his parents made their own diagnosis: they believed Mateo was suffering from mal de ojo. They arranged for him to see a local *curandero*—a shaman or healer with intimate knowledge of native folk practices.

Mateo reluctantly met with the curandero. He was led into a back room in the curandero's cottage where the two sat on the floor. Mateo, who was still suffering from his mysterious illness, was unsurprised when the curandero quickly told him he was suffering from "a bad case of mal de ojo."

They didn't spend much time talking. Almost immediately the *curandero* began a ritual he claimed would cure Matteo of his illness. "He told me that my spirit was sick, and that the sickness was simply manifesting itself in my body. I'd been raised with that kind of thinking, but I still didn't believe his ritual would do anything."

The ritual was a *limpia*—a spiritual cleansing aimed at ridding the body, mind, and spirit of negative energy caused by witchcraft, black magic, or the Evil Eye.

"The curandero started by blessing me with a prayer," Mateo explained. "Then he took a bundle of herbs and moved it around my body and kind of batted it against specific areas of my body as he prayed. He held it to my chest—my heart—for a good long while, and then he did the same thing with my head. I didn't close my eyes and I couldn't really bring myself to relax, not at first. I remember feeling the weight of the herb bundle on the back of my neck and taking a deep breath. Being able to take a deep breath without struggling, I mean."

That, Mateo said, was a pivotal moment.

"I didn't believe I was being healed, but I sensed something inside of me shift. Open up. I remember thinking that it felt like a small balloon had popped and released a bunch of pressure from between my shoulder blades. After that I just observed the curandero as he did his thing. He burned incense and started rolling an egg over my body."

The use of an egg for spiritual cleansing is common in many folk magic traditions; an egg represents the womb and fertility and, by extension, birth. In Mateo's case, it represented rebirth. Copal incense wafted around him as the curandero continued praying.

"I don't remember how long it took because by that point in the ritual I really felt relaxed," Mateo said. "I closed my eyes and kind of let go. The strangest thing was that I started crying. That was totally unexpected. I had been sad and frustrated for weeks,

I'm not an emotional person. So it came as a shock to me when tears started rolling down my face. I inhaled the incense and just kept asking to be healed."

Mateo also described being sprayed with something. He felt a misty coolness touch his forehead and arms. Later he learned that it was mescal, an alcoholic beverage derived from the agave plant which is used in a *limpia* to realign the spirit and the body.

When Mateo opened his eyes, he realized he was standing up, which he didn't remember doing. Looking around the room, he saw that the curandero had lit a few white candles. The curandero walked around Mateo while holding one candle, which he then handed to Mateo before he gave him another blessing.

When the ritual was done, Mateo and the curandero spent time talking. Mateo equated the conversation to "a therapy session with a lot of soul." The curandero assured Mateo that his physical symptoms would soon dissolve.

"I definitely felt different when I left the curandero's house," Mateo said. "I wasn't healed—not by a long shot. I actually had a tough time just sitting in the back of my parents' car because of the pain in my back. But the anxiety was pretty much gone. That much I know."

That night, Matteo slept peacefully. It was the first time he had done so in several weeks. Three days after the limpia ritual, he woke up without any pain and had a voracious appetite.

"I can't explain it scientifically, but I was definitely cured. I think of myself as having been healed of the mal de ojo," Matteo explained. "After I got back to my own house and went back to work, I did a lot of research about *curanderismo* and many of the magical traditions that are native to Mexico and much of Latin America, and when you get down to the base of it, what you find is that they're all really about healing. The word *healing* has a different meaning for me now."

Malocchio: The Evil Eye in Italian Culture

In both Italian and Italian-American culture, the Evil Eye is known as malocchio, which literally translates to "bad eye." I was blessed to grow up in a home where the rituals to diagnose and cure it were performed all the time and for many people. But not until I was in my early twenties did I realize that malocchio rituals differ greatly among Italians and Italian-Americans. My maternal grandparents, as well as my mother, were born and raised in the Province of Caserta. There, in the Campania region of Italy, the towns and villages dotting the mountainous landscape share deep-rooted similarities, as well as many differences. The dialects that are spoken in the region mostly derive from Neapolitan dialect, but every village has its own unique language. Though I speak the dialect my grandparents spoke, many of the words and phrases that are familiar to me might not make sense to someone who speaks a dialect from a town a few miles away.

Let's say a person from the Campania region comes up to me and says: "Hey, Antonio. I hear your family is from Gallo Matese." I nod, and then reply: "Yes, my mother and grandparents were born in *Ru Ualle.*" Ru Ualle is the dialectical term for Gallo Matese; it's known to, and used mostly by, people who were born in Gallo or were raised speaking its dialect.

So it is with malocchio. The "so-close-but-so-different" syndrome is common all over Southern Italy. My father was born in Bari, located in the Apulia region, and though I speak Italian fluently, I can barely understand the *Barese* dialect. There are beautiful folk magic traditions from the Apulia region; I know of two malocchio rituals and several warding techniques that are uniquely *Pugliese*, and most of them differ significantly from those practiced in Campania.

There's a common belief that only women perform the rituals to cure and diagnose malocchio. This is false. In the town of my maternal grandparents, women were certainly regarded as powerful practitioners, but when people felt afflicted by bad luck or inexplicable illness, they often visited a *magone* (pronounced *mah-go-nay*)—a male magical practitioner. In Italian, a *mago* is a male healer and a *maga* is a female healer. Both are accomplished and well-versed in their respective practices, but how each one tackles the problem of malocchio depends on the region of Italy from which they hail. My grandmother used water, oil, and a secret prayer. Today my aunt and sister use the same exact ritual. Someone from the nearby town of Letino, however, might perform the ritual with a different prayer while using a pair of scissors or a knife.

Another commonly held belief is that the malocchio ritual or prayer can only be handed down to someone on Christmas Eve. Again, this is false. Clinging to these steely ideas detracts from what the Evil Eye truly is—a global and multicultural practice. Many of the Italian and Italian-American practitioners I interviewed did not inherit the ritual on that sacred night, and all were adamant that this doesn't mitigate its efficacy. Incidentally, receiving the ritual on Christmas Eve isn't necessarily a formal or elaborate experience. Some learn it at a kitchen table while sauce is simmering on the stovetop. Others memorize the prayers or incantations just before heading to Midnight Mass, where they are instructed to make a specific gesture or intone a specific word at the exact moment when transubstantiation occurs. (A Christmas Eve malocchio ritual can be found on page 130.)

Carlo, a practitioner who was born in Sicily, immigrated to Canada as a child and has spent most of his life in Toronto. When he was in his twenties, his father passed on to him their family's tradition to diagnose and cure malocchio. This did not occur on Christmas Eve but rather on the feast day of a particular saint (of which Carlo refused to disclose).

"I was taught to start the ritual with salt," he explained. "That's the first ingredient. I grab the salt before I even fill a bowl with water and reach for olive oil. Then comes the prayer, which I have to say three times. If I see that malocchio is present, I use that water to bless the person for whom I'm doing it, and I bless them three times. I make a cross over their eyes, over their hands, and their chest. If the person isn't physically there with me—which happens a lot—I have to recite the prayer while thinking of them."

As with most folk magic practitioners, Carlo does not reveal the prayers taught to him by his father. "The prayers are definitely old, and not things you'd recite in church," he said. "But they're Catholic. Would a priest approve of them? No. Do I care what a priest thinks about malocchio or the ritual I use to break it? No. In Sicily, it was the regular folk who did the healing and chased away the devil, not the priests."

From her kitchen in New Jersey, Jennifer often detects and cures malocchio the way her grandmother did decades ago. "I always say that I do it *Calabrese* style," she said, referring to Calabria, the region in Italy where her father was born. "First, I have to say two prayers out loud, and I say them in Italian. I ask the person I'm trying to help to sit down so that I can bless them while I'm praying. I fill the water bowl and pass the bowl over the person's head, then I drop olive oil into the water. Depending on what I see in the bowl, I'll empty it out, refill it, and then pass it around the person's shoulders and their head again. All of this is done while reciting prayers."

Jennifer confirmed that she does not—nor did her grandmother—use salt to cure malocchio. She recites Catholic prayers but specifically invokes the Virgin Mary. "A part of one of the prayers has to do with Our Lady of Mount Carmel," Jennifer explained. "I don't think she's the patron of my father's hometown.

I think it's more likely that my family had a devotion to Our Lady of Mount Carmel going way back and somehow it got incorporated into the ritual."

Several years ago, I was handed down two malocchio rituals by a maga whose magic is rooted in both northern and central Italy. What she taught me was a surprise and a revelation. Oil and water form the basis of those rituals, but salt, matches, and specific incantations are also used. There's even an herbal component if the malediction is particularly nasty. Prior to being handed the rituals, I had never heard the incantations and accompanying prayers or seen the anointing methods. But they work.

Evil Eye magic works because its rituals are rooted in old ways, and the words and gestures woven into those ways possess immense power. Sometimes the simplest magic is also the most dynamic.

Matiasma/Mati: The Evil Eye in Greek Culture

In Greece, it's uncommon *not* to see a mati or other protective symbol in someone's home or business. The same is true of Greek-American neighborhoods in the United States. Called *matiasma*, the Evil Eye has been a staple of Greek culture for thousands of years.

Sophia, a resident of New York City, was raised in a traditional Greek Eastern-Orthodox home. When she was in her twenties, her uncle passed on to her a secret prayer that has been in her family for generations—a prayer used solely to remove the Evil Eye.

In Greek tradition, practices to remove the Evil Eye are almost always passed from a male relative to a female relative, or vice versa. Unlike the ritual to diagnose and cure malocchio, which almost always requires water and oil, the ritual to banish matiasma can be accomplished with just a single prayer. Sophia needs no other accoutrements to banish the curse. She acknowledges, however, that this differs from region to region in Greece.

"My family's tradition is to banish the Eye through prayer," she explained. "I have to make the sign of the cross and say the prayer three times while incorporating the name of the afflicted individual."

In that liminal space between spoken prayer and interior silence, the Eye makes itself known to her. She recognizes its presence once she begins to experience physical symptoms. "My eyes will start tearing up right away," she said. "In my family, when we remove the Eye, we take on the negative energy that's afflicting the victim. I can feel it. It doesn't last long, but it's there. I know the Eye has been broken once I start to yawn. That's the first sign that the prayer is working. Then, when the afflicted person yawns, I know the Eye is gone."

That Sophia must absorb the baneful energy in order to banish it is not a common phenomenon among practitioners. Though it sounds terrifying, Sophia has never experienced the lasting effects of bad energy. In fact, the process has only strengthened her faith in the efficacy of the prayer.

"I've experienced it firsthand," she said. "I know it's real. I remember the first time I did the ritual for someone. I remember how it felt. That experience alone dispelled any doubts I might have had about the Evil Eye. How could it *not* be real? Energy is energy, and it's all around us."

Banishing the Eye is only one part of the magic. To ward it away, Sophia uses amulets like blue beads and the traditional mati. She also carries a *filakto*—a small pouch that has been formally blessed by a priest. Originally used to protect infants and children, the filakto is a common protective device among adults in the Greek community. A woman might pin the pouch to her bra, and men carry the pouches in their pockets. Mothers almost always pin a filakto on the back of their children's clothing before leaving the house.

"It's all connected," Sophia said. "The Evil Eye, and the need to protect yourself against it, is deeply ingrained in our culture."

Spit to Transmit: The Power of Your Saliva

There's a scene in the movie *My Big Fat Greek Wedding* that illustrates the cultural resonance of the Evil Eye. When the main character, Toula (played by Nia Vardalos), is walking down the aisle at her own wedding, her Greek relatives on one side of the church intone the sound *"tfu tfu"* as they spit at her dress. Toula is unfazed, but her soon-to-be American in-laws are visibly disturbed. To the untrained eye, it *looks* like Toula's Greek clan is actually spitting on her dress; in reality, they're mimicking the act of spitting. Sure, bits of saliva might slip past their lips and land on her pristine wedding dress, but that's a small price to pay when you consider what's at stake. The Greek guests at Toula's wedding are doing their part to keep envious glances and thoughts from manifesting in the life of the couple. Given the success of the film and its sequel (not to mention the marriage within the movie), I think we can all agree that they succeeded.

The *"tfu tfu"* sound, when combined with the motion of spitting, creates its own kind of marriage—a powerful union in which protection and warding play equal roles. In ancient Greece, "ritual spitting" was practiced to both protect and bless. The Romans also spat three times to chase away bad luck; this practice was called *despuere malum*—to spit at evil. Spitting was considered a curative act in Ancient Egypt. How did Thoth heal Horus's injured eye? By spitting on it! From the Egyptian *Book of the Dead*: "My arrival means that I spit on the innards, bind the arm, raise the thigh. The crew boards as Ra commands."

Pliny the Elder wrote about the power of saliva in his *Natural History*: "A woman's fasting spittle is generally considered highly efficacious for bloodshot eyes." Pliny also promoted spittle against the dangers of snakes and praised the use of "fasting spittle"— saliva obtained from a person who is actively fasting. In the Bible, Jesus mixes his spittle with mud and then uses the clay-like substance to restore sight to a blind man. Another example comes from Mark 7: 32–35: "And they bring unto him one that was deaf, and had an impediment in his speech; and they beseech him to put his hand upon him. And he took him aside from the multitude, and put his fingers into his ears, and he spit, and touched his tongue; And looking up to heaven, he sighed, and saith unto him, Ephphatha, that is, Be opened. And straightaway his ears were opened, and the string of his tongue was loosed, and he spake plain."

In Islam, spitting is also believed to have magical properties. *Sahih al-Bukhari*, Volume 4, Book 54, Number 513, states the following: "A good dream is from Allah, and a bad or evil dream is from Satan; so if anyone of you has a bad dream of which he gets afraid, he should spit on his left side and should seek refuge with Allah from its evil, for then it will not harm him."

Nowadays, spitting at someone seems a strange thing to do. It's a sign of disrespect and, in some places, a crime. But that hasn't stopped the practice from staying put in certain cultures. While it's not so common to hear about someone being cured of an ailment after getting hit in the face with a frothy wad of spit, it *is* common to see and hear about people spitting to ward away evil and bad luck. This is certainly true in Italian culture. In many parts of Southern Italy, a parent, grandparent, nurse—or any adult, for that matter—will spit (usually three times) on the ground if the child in their care receives a compliment. In Jewish culture, spitting three times while saying "pooh, pooh, pooh!" or "*tfu, tfu, tfu*" is an old practice believed to send demons (and the Evil Eye) fleeing. In Romania, it was once a regular practice to spit in order to avoid deochi—the Evil Eye. In parts of North India, mothers spit to one side of their children so that the Eye will look the other way and not harm them.

So, what's the origin and reason behind saliva's power? Throughout history, bodily fluids were believed to hold tremendous spiritual power, and this is still true today. In many magical traditions, blood, semen, and urine are used in love spells, protection spells, healing spells, and curses. Why should saliva be any less potent? If the eyes are the windows to the soul, the mouth can be considered the doorway to the soul. It's through the mouth that we breathe, eat, and communicate. The most common way to express an emotion—be it anger or love—is via the mouth. We kiss. We smile. We laugh. We scream. We rant. We sing. We gasp. We bite. And we spit.

The act of spitting three times can be tied to the fact that three is a mystical number, representing completion and unity. When it comes to warding, spitting three times is shielding the body, the mind, and the spirit.

Zoroastrianism and the Evil Eye

Believed to be one of the world's oldest religions, Zoroastrianism is based on the teachings of Zoroaster, an Iranian prophet. It is a monotheistic faith rooted in the worship of a benevolent deity known as Ahura Mazda (Lord of Wisdom). Its most significant sacred text is the *Avesta*, which comprises Zoroaster's numerous teachings. At the core of Zoroastrianism is the belief that creation is pure; everything should be treated with love and respect, especially the natural environment. To pollute a body of water, any land, or the air itself is considered antithetical to the concept of creation itself. As such, Zoroastrianism has been called the world's first ecological religion.

Today, the majority of Zoroastrians live in India, Iran, and North America. When it comes to the Evil Eye—or nazar—adherents are known to take strict measures both inside and outside of their homes. Children are taught to eat privately, never in front of strangers, so that nazar (or the demons that accompany it) will be unable to enter their bodies orally. Zoroastrians also believe that a menstruating woman can cast the strongest Evil Eye curse. Bathing is paramount when it comes to removing nazar. Fragrant smoke is also a popular method for cleansing away negativity (page 195); this is usually performed through burning wood, botanicals, and seeds. Fire is considered a great purifier among Zoroastrians.

CHAPTER THREE

AMULETS, TALISMANS, AND HOW TO WARD AWAY THE EVIL EYE

There's a good chance you're wearing one now—an amulet or talisman that represents your desire for protection, good luck, or the powers attributed to a particular deity. Is it a pentagram, the symbol of modern witchcraft? Perhaps it's a cross or a medal of your favorite saint, or a Star of David. Maybe it doesn't have any religious affiliation but is instead a locket that contains a picture of a departed loved one. Humans wear amulets and talismans for a host of reasons and have done so for thousands of years.

Though many people use the words interchangeably, there's a significant difference between an amulet and a talisman. An amulet provides defense from negative energies and situations. A classic example is the nazar, which is worn, carried, or displayed to keep the Evil Eye at bay. The same is true of the Hamsa, also known as the Hand of Fatima, the Hand of Miriam, and the Hand of Tanit. Wearing one of these ancient symbols is an act of magic, for it creates a shield of protection around the individual. An amulet may be inscribed with words or images; some are plain, others elaborately crafted. They can be made of almost any material—steel, iron, clay, stone, glass, plastic, or bone.

A talisman, on the other hand, grants positive energy to the individual wearing it. Think of a horseshoe or rabbit's foot; both are associated with good luck, and whether you hang the former over the front door of your home or carry the latter in your pocket, the goal is the same: to attract advantageous circumstances or radiate a positive vibe. Have you ever brought a "lucky" pen to a job interview? Some people slip a rose quartz into their pocket before going on a first date, hoping to stir up romantic vibrations. Stones like amethyst and tiger's eye are believed to help foster success. The right talisman will assist you in gaining a favorable outcome. But the desired outcome isn't always luck or love; sometimes it's about healing, either physically or spiritually.

Why do we wear amulets and talismans? Most magical practitioners can answer this question with a high degree of knowledge and passion because the subject matter is woven into the fabric of our everyday lives. We use amulets and talismans to feel empowered, safe, anchored, cleansed. More specifically, we use amulets to honor deities, summon spirits, commune with the dead, ward away negative energy and the people who want to project that energy on us. I am a devotee of the goddess Hekate, and among the many amulets I wear is the Wheel of Hekate; sometimes I also wear a skeleton key, as it's a symbol closely linked to the great goddess of the crossroads.

Do I believe amulets and talismans posses power? Indeed, I know they do.

Historically, the psychology of amulets and talismans hasn't changed very much. Protective devices have been used for thousands for years and were not only worn on the body; they were etched onto large stone slabs, ships, the facades of structures, and Egyptian coffins. The symbols and images that became amulets can still be found lining the walls of caves all over the world. The human eye has an extensive history as a symbol of protection dating all the way back to Antiquity. Names, images, and prayers differ from one system of spiritual beliefs to another, but the use of amulets doesn't.

SELECTED AMULETS AND TALISMANS

Today we use amulets and talismans for the same reasons our ancestors did: to ward away negative forces (mainly the Evil Eye) and to attract positive forces. In theory, it sounds simple. In reality, it isn't—or, to be more specific, it isn't merely a matter of purchasing an amulet, looping a chain through it, and wearing it around your neck. Taking action to defend yourself, your loved ones, and your possessions against any type of energy is a form of defensive magic. And what, precisely, is "defensive magic?" It's a way, or a series of ways, to protect yourself. Remember when you moved in to your house or apartment? You probably changed the locks or installed an alarm. Maybe you added a light source to a dark walkway or foyer. Defensive magic is much the same thing: it's about taking steps to ensure your personal safety in a world where just about anything can happen.

If you are of the belief that you don't need to employ warding techniques or any additional methods because your daily meditation or prayer practice already provides you with ample protection, please read the following sentence slowly and thoughtfully: **You can never be too safe.** This is true in the mundane world, and it's also true in the spiritual world. Crimes happen in even the most expensive neighborhoods. If you're spending a cool million to live in an exclusive enclave, you're doing so with the expectation that danger can't touch you, or that the probability of encountering danger is substantially lower in your high-class digs than it is in other, less affluent areas. That's only true to a certain degree. A person armed with determination and just a bit of skill will find a way to dodge or outsmart the cameras, the alarm system, the security guard, and your deadbolt. Not all of the time, but some of the time. So what do you do? Is there even a point to those high-tech security measures and self-defense classes? Of course there is—they add strong layers of protection to your life, and most of the time they *do* work. But too often, we get complacent with the big picture and forget about the little details. And sometimes the little details are portals to big problems.

The same applies to the spiritual world—which, incidentally, is not "somewhere out there" or beyond the beautiful sunsets and the moonlit meadows. The spiritual world exists right beside our own, like the parallel lane of a highway. It's as close to us as our breath. Those of us who practice folk magic, witchcraft, daily prayer, or any methods that link us to the unseen world can also get comfortable in the belief that our spells, meditations, and protection candles make us immune to harm. That's not the case. Just like the determined burglar who will find a way in to a highly secured house, a person's seething jealousy, envy, or resentment will sometimes slip past our magical workings and into our lives. We all know deeply spiritual people who have suffered the impact of the Evil Eye. I believe it happens to all of us at some point in our lives. This doesn't make our magic or prayers less effective. It simply means that we have to reconfigure and recalculate our spiritual strategy. An amulet or talisman can help accomplish that.

As I mentioned earlier, utilizing the power of amulets requires more than just wearing them. As you read through the following list of amulets and talismans, pay attention to which one "clicks" with you. Approach the process with an open mind and put aside any preconceived notions about what you *should* be doing. In other words, don't think that you have to choose a cross or saint medal as an amulet just because you're Catholic or were raised a Christian. Don't choose a Star of David just because you're Jewish. Let your intuition guide you.

The Evil Eye

I feel very connected to the amulets I wear. I understand my intense devotion to Saint Therese of Lisieux—I went to Catholic school and have had a series of extraordinary experiences with her—but my devotions to Papa Legba, Marie Laveau, and Hekate are a bit of a mystery. The first time I saw a *veve* of Papa Legba and put it on, I felt something inside of me shift. I had the same experience the first time I lit a candle for Marie Laveau, and the first time I went to a crossroads to recite an incantation to Hekate. I wear amulets with their images or symbols because I feel a visceral connection to them.

The power of an amulet or talisman is especially strong when you're linked to it, either visually or through its history and meaning. The nazar is the most popular Evil Eye amulet, but an Eye of Horus might resonate more deeply with you. Look closely at the images. Read the descriptions. When one (or two or three) makes your heart beat a little faster, acknowledge the feeling—it's your intuition guiding you. The protection that a particular amulet can provide is the protection you either need right now or will need in the near future.

Azabache Stone

Also known as jet, the Azabache stone is black and very shiny when polished. The stone is either carried on its own as an amulet or is affixed to bracelets, pendants, necklaces, earrings, and pins. It is among the most popular stones throughout Latin America because of its power to ward against the Evil Eye. Those who wear the stone believe it absorbs all forms of negative energy. In Cuba, bracelets adorned with Azabache stones and red coral are placed on the wrists of infants; sometimes a gold pin with the stone is affixed to an infant's clothing. Crosses, hands, figurines, and other shapes are commonly carved from Azabache. The stone is also used for the healing of illness or injuries attributed to the Evil Eye.

If placing an Azabache stone amulet on the wrist of an infant or child, or if you wear one yourself, pay close attention to it—small cracks that appear in the stone are indications that the Evil Eye was aimed at you but successfully averted. If the amulet breaks, the Eye's curse was particularly strong.

The Cimaruta

In Italian, *cima di ruta* means "top of rue," referring to the upper part of the rue plant. This amulet is, in fact, a sprig of rue from which several other branches sprout. Attached to each branch is an apotropaic device, among them a rooster, a key, a snake, a hand, a blade, a crescent moon, a fish, and other symbols. The *cimaruta* is essentially several amulets within a single amulet. It is used to impede the Evil Eye but also acts as a talisman; in Italian it's referred to as a *portafortuna*—a "luck bringer" or lucky charm.

There is debate about the cimaruta's origins. Some scholars give a nod to the theory that it is an ancient charm from the region of Southern Italy, while others believe it is a more "modern" symbol worn by Italian-American witches. In *The Cimaruta and Other Magical Charms from Old Italy*, the late Raven Grimassi theorized that the amulet has ties to antiquity. Similarly, Frederick Thomas Elworthy in his book *The Evil Eye: The Classic Account of an Ancient Superstition*, published in 1895, compares the cimaruta to an early Etruscan amulet he saw displayed in the Bologna Museum, and states that it is reasonable to conclude that the cimaruta was, at the very least, inspired by amulets from antiquity.

Whether the cimatura's roots are ancient or modern has no bearing on its power as an amulet to ward away the Evil Eye. Those who wear a cimaruta believe that its multiple branches and symbols grant it extra potency.

Cornicello (Corno)

In Italian culture, the *cornicello* is by far the most popular amulet to thwart malocchio. It is also referred to as a corno or *cornetto*. Upon seeing a cornicello around someone's neck, your first thought might be: *Why am I looking at a red horn or pepper?* Several years ago, the comedian Sebastian Maniscalco gave the world a funny anecdote about the cornicello during one of his stand-up performances. (Incidentally, Maniscalco also discussed the Evil Eye with Jimmy Kimmel on *Jimmy Kimmel Live* in 2018.) When he was a young adult, Maniscalco drove his first car to pick up a girl. Upon entering the vehicle, the young woman said: "Why the hell is there a red pepper hanging from the rearview mirror?" Most Italian-Americans have had a similar experience. The word "cornicello" means "little horn" and is traditionally carved from red coral. Red is believed to be the color of victory over one's enemies *and* victory over Satan, who is frequently depicted with red skin or glowing red eyes. Today a cornicello can be made of silver or gold. Depending on the vendor, you may even find one fashioned from good old rubber.

Use of the cornicello as an amulet is believed to have begun in the Mediterranean region during the Neolithic period (around

3,500 B.C.E.), clearly pointing to its pre-Christian roots. A fairly common theory interprets the cornicello as being symbolic of an animal's horn—a weapon of protection and self-defense. Another theory is that the cornicello has ties to the lunar goddess, to whom horns were sacred. Additional archaeological evidence dates the cornicello—or the use of horns as apotropaic devices—to Roman times.

It is a common practice among Italians, Italian-Americans, and Italian-Canadians to gift a cornicello to newborn babies, as they are thought to be particularly susceptible to the Evil Eye. Some families, depending on the region of Italy from which they come, will pin the amulet to a baby's clothing either immediately before or immediately after his or her baptism.

Phallic in shape, the cornicello has a special place around the necks of Italian men; the amulet stifles malocchio while simultaneously ensuring virility and fertility. But it isn't solely for wearing around one's neck. Farmers in Italy tie a cornicello to the branches of new trees, thereby thwarting the Eye's effects. Similarly, tying a cornicello to a car's rearview mirror is believed to neutralize the Eye and ensure safe travels.

Evil Eye Beads

For countless decades, the blue-and-white color scheme of the nazar has been a global representation of the Evil Eye and the amulet most people use to combat it. In recent years, however, different colors have been added to the original motif, ushering in a new wave of Evil Eye jewelry aesthetics. But the colors are more than just eye candy; each hue is linked to a purpose and an intention, making the nazar magically multifunctional. Here is a list of color correspondences that will help you streamline your own amulets and how you choose to enhance your protection.

Orange: Helps bolster confidence, especially when pursuing a creative project or goal.

Dark blue: To induce serenity, comfort, and communication. Deflects negativity.

Turquoise: Wear or hang to bring peace, especially in the home and during stressful times; expanding your spiritual outlook.

Green: Abundance, growth, and to bring about equilibrium in relationships.

Purple: To remove obstacles and expand on professional ideas and goals; excellent for business matters.

Amber: Provides protection and fosters a deeper connection to nature and the element of earth. Also helps create order out of chaos.

Red: Enhances strength and courage, especially when dealing with personal matters. Also promotes fertility and is excellent for protecting against the Eye in matters relating to love and sex.

Yellow: Ensures vitality and robust health. Aids in enhancing focus and boosting mental stimulation.

Pink: Keeps meaningful relationships safe from envy and manipulation. Promotes an overall sense of serenity and well-being. A good color to foster greater self-confidence, self-love, and all manner of self-care.

White: Stimulates focus; helps in spiritual cleansing for home and office. Also symbolizes new beginnings and wealth.

Light Green: Promotes success in all ventures. Protects success from envy and greed. Symbolizes vitality, virility, and overall contentment.

Black: Provides protection against envy, malice, negative forces, and curses. Fosters spiritual strength. Protects against psychic vampires and attacks. Helps avoid obstacles.

Eye of Horus

One of the most recognizable amulets in the world, the Eye of Horus symbolizes protection, prosperity, and strength; for some, it is a talisman that brings healing and renewal during life's darker times.

Egyptian mythology tells us interesting (but slightly differing) tales about this ancient symbol. The god Osiris is killed by his own brother, Set, who quickly assumes power. Then Osiris's son, Horus—whose eyes are believed to have represented the sun and moon—wages war on his uncle. Following a series of battles, Horus triumphs, but only after he loses an eye to Set. (In other versions of the myth, Horus gouges out his own eye in an act of sacrifice to bring his father back.) Later, the lost eye is magically restored by either Hathor or Thoth.

The Eye of Horus is a symbol not only of protection, but also rejuvenation, victory, and the might of the warrior. It can quickly distract or entirely stop the Evil Eye in its tracks. Men often wear this amulet to enhance virility and gain "sight" into relationship problems that arise between fathers and sons. For women, the Eye of Horus provides insight when it comes to matters relating to fertility.

Faravahar

A winged sun disk with a male figure in its center, Faravahar is the symbol most associated with Zoroastrianism today, representing for its adherents God, or Ahura Mazda. The ancient symbol's definitive meaning, however, is unknown. Modern theories hypothesize that Faravahar may also signify *fravashi*—personal spirit or a guardian angel. Other new age interpretations delineate the symbol piece by piece: the human figure that stands in the center of the disk is the soul, and the figure's upward-pointing hand a metaphor for spiritual development and a reminder of higher powers at work; the circle itself, or the sun, is immortality; the figure's wings are comprised of three rows of feathers that signify good thoughts, good words, and good deeds; the figure's tail, also containing three rows of feathers, represent bad thoughts, bad words, and bad deeds; the two streamers at the bottom of the symbol are the spirits of good and evil, or the choice all humans must make on a daily basis. More general interpretations view Faravahar as the soul as it departs the complex web of humanity.

Faravahar is linked to ancient Persia, but many scholars claim that the symbol likely originated in Mesopotamia. It can be found among the ruins of Persepolis (the capital of the Achaemenid Empire) in Iran, and on architecture in Egypt, Assyria, and Babylonia. Wearing a Farahavar amulet is beneficial because it ensures a life closely connected to divinity, and thus protected from all danger and evil—especially the insidiousness of the Evil Eye.

Hamsa (The Hand)

Also known as the Hand of Fatima and the Hand of Miriam, the hamsa is a pan-Semitic symbol of protection, unity, and strength. The shape of an open palm, it may have roots in ancient

Carthage (modern day Tunisia), as well as the Iberian Peninsula, North Africa, Portugal, and Spain. Some believe the earliest use of the Hamsa as an amulet can be traced to Mesopotamia in 4,000 B.C.E., which many scholars believe would link it to the goddess Ishtar. It may also be linked to the Hand of Tanit, an image used by the Phoenicians to deflect evil.

The hamsa is inextricably bound up in the theory of the hand itself having spiritual power. The hand can bestow a blessing or a curse; it can heal, harm, or prevent harm.

How did the hamsa become known as the Hand of Fatima? Islamic folklore offers the following tale. One day Fatima was cooking in her kitchen when her husband, Ali, came home with another woman. Stunned, Fatima dropped the soup ladle she had been using. She was too rattled to notice that she had done so and continued stirring the soup with her bare hand. Consumed by emotional pain, she didn't notice the physical pain of her burning hand. Ali soon recognized his mistake and returned his love and devotion to Fatima. Thus, the Hand of Fatima is symbolic of loyalty and faith as well as protection.

The Evil Eye

Does the word "hamsa" derive from the Arabic word *khamsa*, the number five? It may also represent the five pillars of Islam: faith, fasting, pilgrimage, prayer, and alms-giving. In Hebrew and Aramaic, *chamesh* translates to the number five and the Torah is comprised of the five books of Moses: Genesis, Exodus, Leviticus, Numbers, and Deuteronomy. The Hand of Miriam refers to Miriam, one of the seven major female prophets of Israel. She was also the sister of Moses, who led the Israelites out of Egypt, and Aaron, the first high priest.

In Hindu and Buddhist faiths, the hamsa (or the hand itself) represents the five senses, as well as the chakras and their associated *mudras* (gestures), which facilitate energy flow in the body. Each finger corresponds to a chakra. The thumb: solar plexus. The index finger: heart chakra. The middle finger: throat chakra. The ring finger: root chakra. The little finger: sacral chakra. In Hindu iconography, Ganesha is often depicted with one hand upraised.

The hamsa also holds significance in Christianity. In Marian art, the Virgin Mary is frequently depicted with an upraised hand. Christians who wear a hamsa may refer to it as the Hand of Mary, and here it becomes an amulet that also represents the mother of Jesus Christ, a woman exalted by God and imbued with tremendous power. If anyone can fight off the Evil Eye, it's Mary.

The eye that appears in the middle of a Hamsa is a reference to both seeing and deflecting the Evil Eye. Other icons have become an accepted part of the Hamsa's design; among them are the Shema (the central prayer and declaration of faith in Judaism), the pentagram , and the cross, as well as fish, lizards, and numerous other motifs.

Like the nazar, the Hamsa's popularity has grown tremendously over the past several years. An emerging theory among those who favor the hamsa as a protective amulet is that wearing it also enhances intuition.

Mano Cornuto

If you fold your thumb over your bent middle and ring fingers while keeping your index and little fingers raised, you have the *mano cornuto*, or the horned hand. The mano cornuto is closely linked to the cornicello; in fact, both amulets are often worn together. Here, the horns aren't ambiguous and can't be mistaken for a red chili pepper. In Italy, if someone thinks they might fall victim to malocchio, they will make this gesture with their right or left hand and say: "Facchio le corna." Translation: *I make the horns.* When the index and little fingers are pointed upward, the gesture is believed to ward away the Evil Eye. However, if one thinks the Eye has already come upon them, the gesture is inverted; using both hands, the index and little fingers are pointed downward while saying "Corna!" or making the sound "tee-yeh!"

Picture yourself sitting at a table in a crowded restaurant with two friends. They're talking about your new motorcycle. All of a sudden, one of them looks at you and says offhandedly: "That's a popular bike. You have to be careful with it." Your response (Italian style) would be to hold up one of your hands and "make the horns," being certain to keep your index and little fingers pointed upward. "Facchio le corna" would be your verbal reply. Your friend doesn't *want* anything bad to happen to you or the bike, but his words are akin to tempting fate. The horns are a defensive gesture, warning the Eye to stay away, just as a bull warns potential prey that he's ready to gore them open.

Stay in the same setting, but imagine a different scenario. You and your friends are talking about your motorcycle, admiring it from the restaurant's window. A waiter comes over to the table and, while setting down your drinks, looks at the bike, then at you, and says: "I've always wanted a Harley-Davidson XR750. It's amazing. But, you know, it's really fast and you have to know how to ride it." As he turns and walks away, your response (Italian-style) is to make the horns with both hands while turning them downward, so that your index and little fingers are pointing at the floor. "Corna!" you say, while jabbing the air in front of and below you. (The sound "tee-yeh" can also be used.) This gesture turns the horns into weapons, stabbing the Eye and poking it out of place. Why? The waiter's comment was laced with envy. In coveting the motorcycle you own, he set the Evil Eye in motion. But with your natural horns, you've thwarted it.

Historically, scholars hypothesize that the gesture as an image and an apotropaic device may be linked to the lunar goddess or the horned god. Today, the mano cornuto is a popular amulet in Italy and in Italian communities worldwide. Men are especially obsessive about wearing one, as it can counteract impotence—when pointed upward, the horns are "erect."

Mano Fico/Figa

The "fig hand" is an old protective amulet and gesture used to ward away the Evil Eye; it's also a very sexually charged one. The amulet's name derives from the Italian word *fica*, which, when translated, refers to the female genitalia, specifically the vulva. The gesture is made by slipping the thumb between the index and middle and fingers of a closed fist, thus representing the act of sexual union. The theory behind the *mano fico/figa* is that the obscenity of the image distracts or diverts the Evil Eye from "seeing" its target. Here, the Eye is directly linked to infertility, especially the ability to cause a man's semen to "dry up." In Italy and Italian communities worldwide, men will quickly make the gesture defensively during an argument, or run out to buy the amulet if they believe someone is specifically targeting their anatomy. (This happens most frequently during disagreements between lovers).

Both the gesture and the amulet can be tied to the Romans, who saw the fig as a symbol of a woman's erotic prowess and her fertility. In mythology, the fig is said to be sacred to Bacchus, though it was also used in ceremonies to honor Dionysus. The fig tree itself represents longevity, happiness, and good luck in several cultures—the very attributes that the Evil Eye seeks to destroy.

Mano Pantea

If you extend the thumb, index, and middle fingers (while keeping the ring and little fingers tucked in), you get the *mano pantea*. It is at once a sign of benediction and a gesture to ward away the Evil Eye. It predates Christianity, but some Christians believe it represents the Holy Trinity and often relegate it to a "priestly blessing" reserved for clerics and other religious. In ancient Egypt it was known as "Two Fingers" and may have represented Isis and Osiris with the thumb signifying their child.

In Italian folk magic, the mano pantea is most frequently used to bestow a blessing on a newborn, an infant, or a child—but the blessing is one of protection, not prosperity. The Holy Trinity is invoked. Jesus, the Virgin Mary, and Saint Joseph are invoked (along with other saints) and a prayer is uttered the keep negative forces at bay and to turn away *le cose brutte*—ugly things.

The Nazar

By far the most common amulet to ward away the Evil Eye, the nazar is comprised of a series of concentric circles in dark blue, white, light blue, and black; in Israel, they are multicolored. When you look at a nazar, you can see the semblance of a human eye: the second circle (white) is the eyeball itself, the light blue circle is the iris, and the black circle is the pupil. Today, the beads are usually made of glass or ceramic and can be worn around the neck or wrist, as well as hung on walls.

No one knows definitively where the nazar originated. What we *do* know is that today it is a favored amulet in many parts of the world. As mentioned earlier, the Greek philosopher Plutarch believed in the theory of extramission, but he also believed that blue-eyed individuals could more readily cast the Evil Eye. Why? Blue eyes were something of a genetic rarity in the Mediterranean

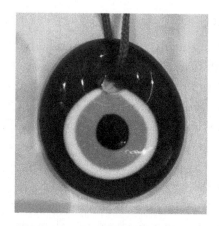

region, and some believe this is the reason for the nazar's striking blue color. If you wear a nazar or carry the beads with you, take notice if one of them cracks—this means the amulet "took the hit" for you and neutralized the negativity.

Ojo de Venado

This amulet is popular among Mexican folk magic practitioners because of its strong protective properties. Its name, when translated, means "deer's eye" and it is fashioned out of red cords and a velvet bean (*mucana pruriens*). The dark bean is said to resemble a deer's eye. Sometimes a tassel is added. It is traditionally placed around a child's right wrist. Some practitioners claim that the bean represents the child and the red cord the child's mother. Many Ojo de Venado bracelets are imprinted with a Catholic image. Like other apotropaic devices, its main function is to ward away mal de ojo. It is not uncommon to see the amulet strung in cars and homes (especially nurseries and children's bedrooms), or worn around the neck.

Om/Aum Symbol

A sound often heard during meditation, Om/Aum has ancient roots in Hinduism, Buddhism, and Jainism. It is referred to as the foundation of Hinduism, as the symbol represents the union of mind, body and spirit. Om/Aum also signifies the supreme being (*parabrahman*), and consciousness (*paramatman*). It is a part of many mantras and can be found in the Vedas and the Upanishads, as well as other Hindu texts.

Each of the symbol's unique curves has meaning: the lower left curve is consciousness; the top left curve is the unconscious state; the lower right curve is the dream state; the semicircle at the top is illusion, believed by many Hindus to be the greatest challenge of the spiritual path; the dot at the top is transcendence and enlightenment. When worn as an amulet, the Om/Aum symbol is protective and facilitates balance and spiritual equilibrium.

Pentagram and Pentacle

The symbol of modern witchcraft, paganism, and Wicca, the pentacle is a five-pointed star within a circle; it represents the four elements—earth, air, fire, water—surmounted by Spirit, or the Goddess and God. The circle refers to totality, harmony, and the cyclic progression of the four seasons (and the seasons of life). When we look at a pentacle, what do we see? Ourselves, of course!

The pentacle is a visual metaphor for the human body, with arms outstretched and legs slightly parted. It represents our dual nature as physical and spiritual beings.

While many people think the words *pentacle* and *pentagram* are interchangeable, they are not; the former is a star within a circle, the latter is a five-pointed star without a circle. Both can serve as either an amulet or a talisman, as each provides protection and fosters spiritual growth while also serving as a tool for evocation. In the 1960s, the pentagram (and, because of its obvious visual similarity, the pentacle) was reviled as a symbol of evil and the "satanic panic" of that time. Though much has changed, many witches, pagans, and other magical practitioners who wear the pentacle as a symbol of faith and as an amulet for protection still have to explain its true meaning to an uninformed public.

Interestingly, there was a time when the pentagram was viewed as a wholly benevolent symbol. It can be dated back to Mesopotamia, where the symbol was inscribed on numerous artifacts. In ancient Greece, it is believed by some that the pentagram was revered for its mathematical perfection. There is also a theory that ancient Hebrews used the pentagram to represent Pentateuch, the first five books of Holy Scripture. Christianity has ties to the pentagram as well—it was a prominent symbol after Jesus Christ's death. Early Christians looked at the pentagram and saw the five wounds Jesus suffered on the cross as well as the Star of Bethlehem. Pentagrams still appear on church facades. The most prominent is the pentacle at the Parish Church of Saint Barnabus in Bethnal Green, London.

Today, witches, Wiccans, and pagans wear the pentacle as a symbol of faith but also to keep all forms of negative energy at bay. Both the pentacle and the pentagram bring about order and stability by harnessing the natural magic of our environment.

The Red String

Some will tell you the red string (or scarlet thread) can be traced back to the Bible. Others only know it as popularized by celebrities with an interest in Kabbalah, leading some cynics to view it as "just another Hollywood fad." Whether you believe the former or the latter actually doesn't matter—the red string is among the most popular amulets in the world to ward away the Evil Eye.

Wearing a red string around the left wrist is a Jewish folk custom. From the metaphysical perspective, it is linked to the Kabbalah. The string, usually made of wool, becomes an amulet through the application of it to one's wrist. In addition to providing protection from the Eye, the string is also believed to assist women in matters of fertility and childbirth; here, it is worn around the waist. Another folk belief is that an unmarried woman should wear the red string until it falls off, at which time she will meet the man who is to be husband. In Israel, the red string is common among religious and secular Jews.

The red string is believed to have roots in the Bible via Genesis 38, which focuses on Judah and Tamar and the birth of their sons.

> And it came to pass, when she travailed, that the one put out his hand: and the midwife took and bound upon his hand a scarlet thread, saying, This came out first.
>
> And it came to pass, as he drew back his hand, that, behold, his brother came out: and she said, How has thou broken forth? This breach be upon thee: therefore his name was called Perez.
>
> And afterward came out his brother, that had the scarlet thread upon his hand: and his name was called Zarah.

One way of ensuring—or awakening—the string's power is to wrap it around the tomb of the biblical matriarch Rachel in Bethlehem.

THE RED STRING IN ITALIAN FOLK CUSTOM

An Italian folk custom also utilizes red ribbon or string, which is usually tied into a bow or knot and then pinned to the inside of a child's shirt. This is generally done before an infant's baptism, but many Italians and Italian-Americans continue the tradition well into adulthood: women pin a red ribbon to their bras, men to the insides of their blazers and coats.

The Evil Eye

Saint Medals

In the pantheon of Roman Catholic saints, many are petitioned for protection against evil, and while it might not be explicitly stated, the term "protection from evil" certainly includes the Evil Eye. Numerous saints were fierce warriors who are understandably associated with protection and self-defense. Others led quiet, contemplative lives but battled evil on a grand scale. While the following list is by no means exhaustive, the saints mentioned here are especially noted for their abilities to battle evil and provide protection.

1. **Saint Benedict of Nursia:** When it comes to combating evil, the Saint Benedict Medal is arguably the most favored amulet in Roman Catholicism. Saint Benedict was born to a noble Roman family. At about twenty years of age, he renounced his wealth and went to live in a cave. He is considered the founder of Western monasticism and wrote the Rule of Saint Benedict, which instructs members of monastic orders on how to live and work while keeping prayer at the very center of their lives. Benedict was a frequent target of

demonic attacks and is thus considered especially effective in fighting evil. Both the medal and an accompanying prayer are sometimes used in the Rite of Exorcism.

The Saint Benedict Medal can be worn as an amulet but is frequently hung above the front doorways of homes and even placed in the foundations of buildings before the actual construction work begins. The medal is elaborate in design and inscription. Whether you choose to wear it or hang it in your home (or both), it's important to understand what's written on the medal. On the front of the medal: *Crux Santi Patris Benedicti.* Translation: Cross of the Holy Father Benedict. The words around the margin of the medal: *Ejus in obitu nro praesentia muniamor.* Translation: May we at our death be fortified by his presence. On the back of the medal: *C.S.S.M.L.—N.D.S.M.D. Crux Sacra Sit Mihi Lux.* Translation: The holy cross be my light. *Non draco sit mihi dux.* Translation: Let not the dragon be my guide. The circles by the four corners of the cross: *CS PB. Crux Sancti Patris Benedicti.* Translation: Cross of the Holy Father Benedict. The initials around the perimeter of the medal: *VRSNSMV—SMQLIVB. Vade Retro Satana, Nunquam suade mihi vana—Sunt Mala Quae Libas, Ipse venena bibas.* Translation: Step back, Satan, do not suggest to me thy vanities—evil are the things though profferest, drink thou thy own poison. At the top of the medal: *PAX.* Translation: Peace.

2. **Saint Joan of Arc:** The young peasant girl from France who led the French army to victory at Orleans is a French national heroine and an international icon of courage, skill, and the enduring power of faith. Joan claimed to have received visions and auditory messages from the Archangel Michael,

Saint Catherine of Siena, and Saint Margaret urging her to liberate France from English domination. After her capture and at her trial, she exuded remarkable poise and strength and never faltered in her devotion to Jesus Christ. She was burned at the stake on May 30, 1431. Later, her conviction was overturned. Though she wasn't officially canonized until 1920, she has been a figure of inspiration and admiration for centuries.

Saint Joan of Arc is synonymous with protection, battle, and all forms of defense. Sometimes *admitting* that you need or want protection is the first step to actually getting it, and that's where Saint Joan plays an especially significant role. She values honesty and understands the old adage "to thine own self be true." A careful review of her life story shows that she had remarkable vision—the power to see what isn't there to be seen. Despite seemingly insurmountable obstacles, her eyes saw victory. Wearing a medal of Saint Joan of Arc ensures that she will remain at your side and assist you in any battle.

3. **Padre Pio (Saint Pius of Pietrelcina)**: A Franciscan Capuchin friar, Padre Pio is among today's most popular saints. His cult is international and numerous miracles have been attributed to his divine intercession. He was born in the Province of Benevento, Italy, in 1887 and entered religious life in 1903. He fell ill early in his priesthood, and many believe that this period marked the beginning of a series of supernatural events that would go on to define his life. Several of his fellow Franciscans witnessed him levitating and in ecstasy. Later, he reportedly manifested numerous spiritual gifts, among them the stigmata and bilocation—the ability to appear in two places simultaneously. It is also widely believed

that Padre Pio did battle with the devil himself. He described being tormented by demonic forces, his flesh bruised from the physical attacks. For this reason alone, he is often petitioned for protection against all manners of evil. Wearing a medal of Padre Pio can trick the Evil Eye into seeing you in two places at once, thereby impeding its trajectory.

The Scarab

Ancient Egyptians held the scarab beetle in immensely high regard, so much so that the insects were placed in tombs or within a mummy's wrappings as part of funerary rites. It was believed that the deceased wouldn't be able to find their way in the afterlife without the aid of the scarab. It might sound odd, but the Egyptians viewed the insect as a symbol of rebirth and resurrection. Why? The beetle rolled its dung into a ball and buried it in the earth so that it could later be used as a source of nourishment for its larvae, thereby illustrating the unending cycle of life. The scarab was also linked to the sun god Khepri, who pushed the sun up over the horizon to begin each new day. Thus, the scarab became synonymous with regeneration and resurrection.

The scarab was also an important amulet for protection to Egyptians, believed to guard them from illness during life and also

to watch over their souls after death. It is still considered a powerful amulet for protection today; wearing it combats the various physical afflictions that accompany Evil Eye sickness.

Star of David

One of the most recognized symbols in all of Judaism, the Star of David is a hexagram that forms a six-pointed star; it is comprised of two overlaid equilateral triangles. In Hebrew, it is referred to as *Magen David*, which literally translates to "shield of David," not "Star of David." This alone gives us a clear indication of the amulet's protective properties. When trying to defend oneself, what better weapon is there than a shield?

The Star of David is believed to have its roots in the Seal of Solomon—which itself was used in mystical rites by Jewish practitioners of Kabbalah, as well as by Muslims. The star signifies God's centrality as ruler of the universe, providing protection from all six directions: north, south, east, west, and up and down. According to the Kabbalah, God created the world using His own seven attributes: *chesed* (kindness), *gevurah* (severity), *tiferet* (harmony), *netzach* (perseverance), *hod* (splendor), *yesod* (foundation) and *malchut* (royalty). These attributes are contained within the Star of David through its six points and its center, the center being yesod, or the focal point from which all else arises.

While there are debates about the origin of the Star of David, it was not until the Middle Ages that the symbol was mentioned in rabbinic literature. A *siddur* (Jewish prayer book) from 1512 has a Star of David on its cover with the following inscription: "He will merit to bestow a bountiful gift to anyone who grasps the Shield of David."

Ta'wiz/Taweez

Worn by Muslims and Hindus, this amulet repels the Evil Eye. When worn as a talisman, it is believed to bring good luck. The most common *ta'wiz* is comprised of a piece of paper that is folded numerous times and then placed inside of a small black pouch to be worn around the neck; on the piece of paper are written (in Arabic) verses from the Quran or the names of Allah. Sometimes a *dua*—a prayer of supplication or a meaningful invocation—is used. The ta'wiz is especially common in South Asia, and those who believe in its power hang it in their homes and around the necks of their children.

There is a debate among Muslims about whether or not it is appropriate or permissible to wear a ta'wiz/*taweez*. Islam views the use of amulets and talismans as superstitious, and such a belief is called a *haram*—an act that is forbidden by God. An extremely large number of Muslims, however, view the wearing of a taweez as permissible.

Takrut

Native to Thailand, the *takrut* is a tubular-shaped amulet believed to provide protection from numerous negative conditions: the Evil Eye, dark spirits, and danger in general. The amulet is usually made of metal or palm leaf and has a scroll-like shape; most takrut contain a *yant*—a small sheet of paper on which invocations, incantations, and sacred geometrical symbols are inscribed. The yant also wards against evil. The amulet is worn around the neck on a cord but can also be tied around one's waist. In certain instances, a takrut is worn close to a particular body part that is believed to either be cursed or to need healing. The origins of the takrut are said to predate the arrival of Buddhism in Thailand. Many believe they are linked to beneficial nature spirits.

There are specific instructions one should follow when putting on a takrut. Anyone wearing the amulet should first wash their hands. Next, they should assume a comfortable position while sitting on the floor or a chair. The amulet should be held in the palm of one hand while pressing the palm of the other hand over it. A suitable mantra should then be selected and chanted. The takrut itself is considered sacred to those who wear it, as it strengthens one's spiritual awareness and physical body.

Tuareg Cross

A lesser-known amulet, the *Tuareg* Cross (also called the Agadez Cross and Cross of Niger) is as enchanting as it is powerful.
The Tuareg people are an ethnic (Berber) confederation found in
Sub-Saharan Africa, mainly in Niger, Algeria, Mali, and Libya,
comprised mostly of artisans and blacksmiths. The unique geometrical design of the Tuareg cross immediately establishes it as a
strong protective symbol, though there is no definitive answer as
to what the cross represents. Some believe it deflects the Evil Eye
via the cross's four arms. Some say the circle at the center of the
cross is a well and the smaller etchings around it the footprints of
the jackals who come to drink at it. Another theory claims that

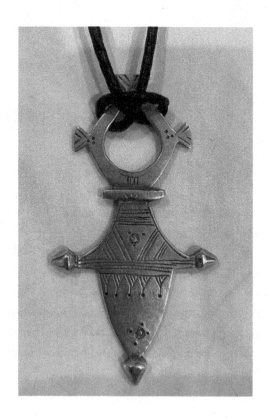

the cross acts as a kind of compass in the Sahara Desert: when aligned with the North Star, it will lead back to Agadez.

As an amulet, the Tuareg Cross safeguards against the Evil Eye and negative energy in general. Because of its unique shape, it is also believed to split and scatter the Eye's baneful energies in all four directions: east, south, north, west.

MAKING YOUR OWN AMULETS AND WARDING DEVICES

The more personal you are with your magic, the more powerful it is. Writing your own prayers, incantations, and spells is a deeply fulfilling experience because it streamlines your intentions and infuses the work with your own unique energy. And so it is with creating amulets. In our consumer-focused world, there's a very good chance you can find an amulet of your favorite deity, saint, angel, or symbol. It would take only a few minutes to go online and buy an amulet of the Archangel Michael, but what if your personal image of him doesn't involve a shield or sword? Maybe you see him as a sphere of blue light instead. When you invoke Hekate, do you picture a misty moonlit crossroads instead of the triple goddess visage?

Making your own amulets depends on your level of craftiness and how much time you're willing to invest in the project. Amulets and talismans are traditionally worn as jewelry, but they are just as potent when carried in your pocket, purse, backpack, or placed in the glove compartment of your car. They don't have to be made of metal or copper or bone. An amulet constructed of paper, ink, glue, candle wax, and a sprinkle of herbs will ward away the Evil Eye just as readily as a nazar. Crafting your own amulet is like designing a room in your home—you choose the colors and fabrics and decide where every last accessory goes, and when it's finished, you can *feel* how connected you are to the space and everything in it.

Stepping into the room empowers you, inspires you, or puts you at ease. You might not like clean lines and bright colors. Maybe dark hues and messier surfaces resonate with you. The point is to create something that you alone understand and appreciate.

An Amulet for an Infant or Child

In Italian and Italian-American communities all over the world, it's common to pin an amulet on a newborn before he or she leaves the hospital. The act is repeated at the infant's baptism and may become a regular practice depending on what region of Italy the family hails from. Incidentally, this is not by any means an "Italian thing." Many cultures use amulets to protect children from the Evil Eye.

The amulets below do not have to be sterling silver; they can be purchased at very little cost from religious goods stores or church shops. To make a general protection amulet you will need:

- A medium or large safety pin

- A red cornicello

- A medal of the Archangel Michael

- A medal of Saint Anthony of Padua

- A short strip of red ribbon or yarn

Gather the items together, either at your altar or your kitchen table. (In many Italian homes, the kitchen table *is* an altar.) Make the sign of the cross. Clasp the medal of the Archangel Michael and recite the Prayer to Saint Michael:

Saint Michael the Archangel, defend us in battle. Be our protection against the wickedness and snares of the devil. May God rebuke him, we humbly pray; And do thou, O Prince of the Heavenly Host, by the power of God, cast into hell Satan and all the evil spirits who prowl about the world seeking the ruin of souls. Amen.

Carefully slide the medal onto the stem of the safety pin. Clasp the cornicello, blow on it, and carefully slide it onto the stem of the safety pin. Clasp the medal of Saint Anthony of Padua and recite the following prayer:

O loving Saint Anthony, you who so clearly heard even the smallest voice and so greatly trusted in God, hear me now. With love and devotion, I ask for your miraculous intercession. Stand before God and ask Him to bless this child [here say the child's name] today. Ask God to keep him/her safe, to protect him/her from illness, disease, and the influence of those who would lead him/her astray. Saint Anthony, stand beside [mention child's name] and help him/her to grow in faith and wisdom, and to become a beloved daughter/son of our Heavenly Father. Shield him/her from the presence and dangers of evil in our world. Amen.

Carefully slide the medal onto the stem of the safety pin. Using both hands, tie a single knot with the red cord or ribbon and recite the following prayer:

Holy Blessed Virgin, who by virtue of your love and strength is a mother to every one of us, hear my prayer: I place this child [child's name] in your care. Shield him/her with your mantle, bless him/her with your gaze, lead him/her away from danger with your loving touch. Vanquish all evil from his/her life, O Holy Mother, today and always. Amen.

Carefully slide the ribbon or yarn onto the stem of the safety pin, making sure to pierce it with the pin's point. The amulet is now ready. It can be used on the day of an infant's baptism by pinning it to the inside of the infant's clothing. It can also be used as a general amulet to ward away the Evil Eye, in which case the amulet should be pinned into the inside of the child's jacket or coat.

A Simple Cord Spell

Knots and cords play a big role in magical practice. They can be used to bless, to bind, to curse, and to ward. A cord and knot spell can also be done spontaneously with the simplest of strings and strong intention. Some people want to use magic but feel uncomfortable using candles, herbs, incense, and symbols, or they may not have the time or space to dedicate to a spell that requires more elaborate effort. That's where cord and knot magic comes in.

This spell is simple and highly effective and takes only a few minutes to cast. The more you use it, the more proficient you will become at performing it. All you need is a string, cord, or ribbon; it can be yarn, satin, silk, or plain thread. Blue, red, and black cords work best for warding.

Get comfortable and hold the cord in your hands. Spend a minute concentrating on warding away the Evil Eye, and be clear about whether the spell is for you, for someone else, or for your home, car, or place of business. When you're ready, recite the following as you tie the first knot: *North, East, South, and West, the circle holds me as I work and rest.* Recite the following as you tie the second knot: *Above, below, and to my left and right, the shield protects me day and night.* Recite the following as you tie the third knot: *Minute to minute, hour to hour, this is my sword, this is my power.*

Carry the cord or string with you as an amulet. You may also place it in your car or hang it in the threshold of your home's front door. Place it on your desk to deflect the Eye at work.

Braid the Prayer into Your Hair

The body itself can be an amulet—especially when we're talking about warding away the Evil Eye. (Let's not forget that the Evil Eye itself makes use of human anatomy.) Body parts have been fashioned into amulets for thousands of years, but in this spell, you're going to use your hair as an amulet to keep envy and its nasty relatives at bay. It's a perfect spell if you find yourself away from home without a more traditional amulet, or if you need to protect yourself with only a few minutes' notice.

This spell is for individuals with long hair. You don't need anything more than a rubber band. Go to a quiet place, whether in your home, office, or car. Begin by making a classic 3-strand braid; you can make the braid as thin or thick as you prefer. As you weave the strands together, recite the following incantation: *One to protect, one to deflect, one to misdirect. When envy comes to seek and find, it won't see me—its eyes are blind.*

Fix the braid with the rubber band and go about your day.

The Hand Encircled

Earlier I wrote about the significance of the human hand as an amulet. Buying and wearing one certainly wards away the Evil Eye, but making one is even more powerful. Your very own hand is unique—no one else in the world has your fingerprints. Our hands receive and project energy, and can serve as weapons at a moment's notice.

Making an amulet out of your handprint is easy. It might seem like a messy art project, but it's actually one of the simplest—and strongest—acts of magical self-defense. It's also something you can do with a partner, housemate, or kids.

You will need:

• Washable paint in color of your choosing

- A sheet of acrylic paper

- Paper plate

- A pinch of rue

- A pinch of salt

- Pen or marker in color of your choosing

- Paper towels or hand towel

After washing and drying your hands, place the sheet of acrylic paper on a hard surface in front of you. Empty the paint onto the paper plate. (If you prefer to be neater, you can also apply the paint directly to your hands with a paintbrush.) Dip your dominant hand into the paint, ensuring that your palm and fingers are fully coated. Then quickly flatten your hand on the paper and hold it there for two or three seconds. When you lift your hand up, there should be a solid imprint on the paper.

Use your other (unpainted) hand to sprinkle the salt and rue directly onto your handprint. After it has dried fully, take the pen or marker and, starting at the top, just above the point of the middle finger, begin writing your name. Write in a continuous circle around the hand so that it's a solid band, literally going all the way around and back to the first point. In the center, or on the palm of your hand imprint, draw a protective symbol—it can be an eye, but it can also be a symbol that has special meaning for you. Do you feel a sense of security when you see a rose or a sword? Do you have a connection with a particular animal? Personalize the imprint to your liking.

When you're done, you can either hang the paper in your home or carry it with you. The first time I made my own Hand Encircled amulet, I taped it to the inside of one of my kitchen cabinets; this ensured that I would see the image every morning when I reached for my coffee mug. I've also kept the imprint on my nightstand and in my car. Many years ago when I started a new job, I made a second imprint, had it laminated, and kept in my briefcase. Whatever you decide, make sure you're in regular contact with the image of your own Hand Encircled. Seeing such a personal imprint sharpens your intuition.

The Nazar Bouquet

The rose is a powerful flower with a long and extraordinary history. In Christianity it is linked to several saints and represents the Virgin Mary as Queen of Heaven. In Islam, the rose symbolizes the Prophet Muhammad. In *The Encyclopedia of Jewish Symbols*, Ellen Frankel and Betsy Platkin Teutsch explain how the rose's blooming process corresponds to the festival of Shavuot. The rose has long been associated with the goddesses Aphrodite and Venus, respectively, and the god Eros.

While looking at a rose or inhaling its beautiful scent instantly conjures images of love and romance, it is also a flower of protection. Have you ever been pricked by a rose? It hurts and usually comes as a great shock. Therein lies the rose's power as a weapon for spiritual defense—it can entice, seduce, and wound all in the same instant.

A nazar bouquet can be used for multiple purposes. When arranged in a vase and kept close to your front door, it wards against the Eye in general; it can also be placed in a nursery or a bedroom for more specific intentions. But the bouquet isn't only for a home. Brides would *especially* benefit from carrying a bouquet that acts as an amulet. This bouquet should be utilized whenever someone moves into a new home or apartment as well.

To create the bouquet, you will need:

- Five blue roses

- Four white roses

- Three light blue roses (if you can't find a lighter hue, using the same color blue is fine.)

- One Black Baccara rose

- A vase filled with water (optional)

- Twine or blue ribbon

- Scissors or gardening shears

You may need fewer or more blue and white roses depending on the size of your arrangement, but you will need only one Black Baccara rose.

Begin by cleaning the stems of leaves and thorns, then trim the stems. (If you're placing them in a vase, it's best to cut at a diagonal.) You want to create a circular bouquet. If you have a particular system of arranging flowers that works for you, by all means use it. I've always found it easiest to begin with the flower that will rest at the center of the bouquet, so take the Black Baccara rose and begin arranging the lighter blue roses around it. Next, arrange the white roses. Last, work the brightest blue roses around the white ones. The arrangement doesn't have to be perfect, but you definitely want the bouquet to resemble a nazar.

Once you've arranged the bouquet to your liking, tie the stems with the ribbon if it's going to be carried. If you work the arrangement into a vase, all you have to do is decide where you want to display it. Remember: there's ancient magic woven into the formation of and colors that comprise the nazar, and that magic will work hard to repel the Evil Eye.

The Table Nazar

It doesn't matter if you're hosting a cozy dinner for three or a party for twenty-five—the Eye is always ready to strike. While this amulet is easy to make, it isn't something you wear; it's meant to be placed on a table or other hard surface and works to absorb or deflect the Eye in your home.

You will need:

- A blue plate (if you don't have one, take a white paper plate and color it blue with paint or marker)

- Salt

- One clove of garlic

- One peppercorn

Before your guests arrive, set the blue plate down on your counter. Slowly pour a ring of salt around the middle of the plate. Place the clove of garlic inside the salt circle. Gently press the peppercorn into the clove of garlic, making sure not to damage the clove. Don't waste time trying to make it look perfect—imperfection is fine.

What kind of event are you hosting? Spend a minute or two thinking about the person or persons who will be sitting at your dinner table, lounging in your living room or on your deck, or traipsing through several rooms of your home. Are any of your imminent guests the envying type? Are any of your friends bringing dates you haven't met yet? Strangers in the house are always a gamble. But instead of worrying, hold your hands above the plate and chant the following incantation: *Eye to eye, and I to Eye, in this scene all is seen. Spirit wakes and envy breaks.*

Place the plate out of eyeshot. Don't hide it in a cabinet or drawer, but don't set it down in the middle of your dinner table either. Use discretion. Find a good place for the plate and let it work its magic. When your guests have left, go to the plate and study it closely. Are there any hairline cracks in the garlic clove? Did the peppercorn fall out of the clove? Is there a break in the ring of salt?

If you find any oddities that weren't there when you set the plate down, the table nazar amulet absorbed the hit. Pour the entire contents of the plate into a trash bag and take it outside. If you don't find any unusual signs in the plate, it's safe to dispose of its contents in a trash bin inside your home. Make this amulet whenever you have guests in your home.

Tie the Red String

Choose a strong red string or piece of cord. You can also purchase a red string from the Tomb of Rachel, the burial site of the biblical matriarch Rachel, located just outside Bethlehem. Many shops and online sites sell (inexpensively) red strings that have been wound seven times around Rachel's Tomb. Once you have procured a red string, follow the following steps.

Choose a person you trust—be it a family member or friend—and together find a place where you can sit in each other's presence, undisturbed, for a few minutes. This can be indoors or outdoors.

When you're ready, hand the string to your trusted friend or family member. Take a minute to focus your attention so that there are only good and loving thoughts between both of you.

Hold out your left arm and ask your friend/family member to tie the string around your wrist, making a single knot as you mentally set your intention. Then ask your friend/family member to tie six more knots with the string. This should be done calmly, and with care, and be certain to keep your thoughts positive during this process. You can pray or meditate. You can also be more direct by vocally "charging" each knot with an intention. For example: "To keep away the Evil Eye. To keep envious people far from me. To strengthen my self-confidence." While this isn't necessary for your red string to be efficacious, many people prefer the path of direct intention.

When the last knot is done, recite the Ben Porat Yosef prayer, which you will read more about later in this book: "Joseph is a fruitful bough, Even a fruitful bough by a well; Whose branches run over the wall." Later, before bedtime, recite the following protection prayer:

In the name of Adonai the God of Israel:
May the angel Michael be at my right
And the angel Gabriel at my left
And in front of me the angel Uriel
And behind me the angel Raphael,
And above my head the Sh'khinah (Divine Presence).

To Ward at Work

The professional environment isn't always a friendly place. Most people have experienced a few work difficulties—bulldozer bosses, cranky coworkers, caustic customers. And, of course, the Evil Eye. If you work from home and think you're safe from the negative vibes of your colleagues, think again. Zoom meetings bring people together in much the same way that a conference room does, thereby exposing you to malevolent stares. The following charm will help you to avert the Eye.

You will need:

- One lime, cut in half

- A glass of water

On the first day of your workweek, place one half of the lime into the glass of water and then set the glass down on your desk. If you don't want coworkers to see it, hide the glass behind a framed picture or a file folder. If you're at home, keep it close to your workspace but out of eyeshot once the Zoom meetings start. It's that simple. Limes have protective properties, so bad juju will be absorbed by the lime and the water. Refresh the glass every two days.

WARDING FOR CHILDREN

- To protect an infant or child from the Eye, a parent should lick his or her thumb three times and make the sign of the cross three times in between the child's eyes and three times on the back of the child's neck.

- Tie a red string on an infant's crib or (to keep the string out of reach and safely away from the child) fasten it high on a wall of the nursery.

- Tie a red string affixed with a nazar or hamsa to a child's stroller. (Always be aware of child safety and do not leave the string where the child can reach it.)

- Anyone who compliments an infant or child should end their sentence with the words "God bless." If an infant or child is complimented and the person fails to do so, spit three times and make the mano cornuto gesture.

- To a small red or blue pouch, a mother or father should add three stands of their own hair, a sprig of rue, and a piece of black tourmaline. Mom should seal the charm by spitting into it three times. (Fingernails can be substituted for hair.)

- Children become immensely attached to certain toys (especially dolls or stuffed animals). To ensure that the Evil Eye has no point of entry, take your child's favorite doll and turn it into a protection charm or amulet. If it's a doll, dab salt into its fake eyes; otherwise, wet the tip of the thumb of your dominant hand and trace an equilateral cross over the toy.

- A stuffed animal with a horn or horns—a unicorn, a goat, a ram, even deer with antlers—will ward away the Eye.

- Depending on your religion or spiritual path, copy your favorite scriptural verse onto a piece of paper that you have cut into a small square. (It should be a verse of protection.) When you're done, slip the paper into an envelope and seal it closed by using your saliva. Tuck the envelope under the child's crib or mattress.

- Sprinkle salt around a child's bed to keep the Evil Eye from working while they sleep.

- Placing a clove of garlic in each corner of a child's bedroom will vanquish lingering envious vibes.

WARDING FOR THE HOME

- Weave (or embed) an image of an eye or a cross into a carpet that will cover any part of the kitchen floor of your home.

- Draw or attain an image of the Eye of Horus and apply it to the bottom of a doormat kept outside your front door. Place the image face-up against the bottom of the mat so that guests unknowingly step on it when they arrive at your front door. This will immediately neutralize their envious thoughts about you and/or your home.

- Place an Evil Eye bead in a glass of water and leave it as close to the front entrance of your home as possible. Empty out the water and refresh the glass every three days.

- Trace the symbol of the sun—a circle with rays emerging from it—into the window frame of the northernmost window of your home to keep the Evil Eye at bay.

- Hang a bunch of chili peppers in the kitchen window. Alternatively, hang a braid of garlic in the kitchen window, or fasten one to the top of the first mirror people see upon entering your home.

- Hang a mirror as close to the front door as possible, preferably within direct eyeshot of the front door so that the Evil Eye will be reflected back on itself before it can unfurl.

- When purchasing a new home, have every member of the family spit three times on the ground outside the front door, then recite the following incantation: *Evil Eyes have no sight—Morning, noon, and every night.*

- Bind three sprigs of rosemary and three sprigs of rue together with red yarn, cord, or ribbon and then fasten the charm to the lintel of your front door with a piece of clear tape.

- When entertaining guests, keep a phallic-shaped object on the kitchen counter or add it to a fruit bowl—a cucumber, a carrot, an eggplant, or a zucchini work best.

ADDITIONAL WARDING TECHNIQUES

- In Italy, it's common for a man to touch or grab his crotch (over his pants) to ward away the Evil Eye. This is done after receiving a compliment that refers to a man's good looks or virility.

- An Armenian practice to counter the Eye: scratch or pinch your butt immediately after receiving a compliment.

- After sneezing, give your right ear a tug so that the Eye won't curse your next compliment or spoken plans.

- Never leave a prayer book open after you're done reading from it. Doing so may invite the Evil Eye into the prayers you recently recited.

- Knock on wood immediately after speaking about specific plans or something positive that you hope will happen. Similarly, touching a piece of iron will counter the Eye.

- Swallowing a whole garlic clove will ward away the Eye. Similarly, carrying an onion in one's pocket will also repel the aftermath of an envious glance.

- To keep a car safe from the Evil Eye, hang a nazar, a hamsa, a rosary, or a saint medal from the rearview mirror. A Saint Christopher medal, the saint of travel safety, is traditionally used for this purpose, but the Archangel Michael also protects travelers.

- Spit once on each car's tires, then moisten the thumb of your dominant hand and trace a triangle over the hood.

- At a wedding, the couple should tie three basil leaves together with a red or blue string and set the talisman between their glasses of wine or champagne.

- Going out to a special event where you might find yourself in the line of Evil Eyes? Carry two bay leaves in your pocket for protection. If, upon returning home, you feel "eyed," burn the leaves immediately.

- If you're with a group of people or even with one person and you feel threatened by envy or someone's heavy stare, create a distraction. Drop your keys or whatever you're holding. If sitting at a table, spill your drink or drop a utensil. If walking around your house with a person or persons in tow, knock something over. The moment of confusion will confuse the Eye.

- At work, keep a rose with thorns on its stem on your desk or in your office; the thorns are believed to stab the Eye before it can hit you. Replace the rose when its petals start drying.

- Mix sea water with a pinch of turmeric and sprinkle in the corners of your home to keep the Eye at bay.

- Immediately after buying a new item, take a coconut and rotate it clockwise over the item seven times. When finished, hold the coconut in between your hands and concentrate on any negative comments or compliments you may have received or believe you may receive. Then smash the coconut on the ground outside of your home.

- Do you need to know if the Evil Eye is harming your business? Place a pumpkin in a corner of your office just outside the front door. If the pumpkin dries out slowly and naturally, the Eye is not present. If the pumpkin "sweats" or gathers moisture, however, the Eye is active and working.

- Use kajal—or black eyeliner pencil—to heavily shadow your eyes before going outside. You can also draw a single black dot in the center of your forehead or on your right cheek.

- Dunk a cotton ball or rag in lavender water and write the word OM (or AUM) on your front door. Ideally this should be done at least once a month.

- Place a handful of uncooked rice and a teaspoon of salt in a small pouch or charm bag (any color). Tie it tightly and carry it in your pocket, purse, or briefcase. If you feel as if you've been hit by the Eye, gently bat the pouch against the back of your neck three times.

CHAPTER FOUR

HOW TO DIAGNOSE
THE EVIL EYE

Do I have it?

Anyone who knows how to diagnose the Evil Eye is intimately familiar with this question—it tends to pop up on an almost daily basis via text or a frantic phone call. Some practitioners are extremely private with their wisdom and never discuss the topic outside of immediate family. Others exercise discretion but extend the magic of what was handed to them beyond their bloodline, offering it to their closest friends and any child in need. Then there are folk witches who want to impart their insight to all those eager to learn. I count myself among the latter bunch. Why? I believe spiritual knowledge leads to spiritual practice, and spiritual practice is an invincible force.

Those unfamiliar with the Evil Eye often become aware of it after enduring an experience that thoroughly spooks them. They've either gone through a scary time or witnessed one at close range. Sometimes watching a friend or family member ride out a bad spell is enough to get you thinking. In my work as both a magical practitioner and a journalist who reports on spirituality and the occult, I've met many people whose perceptions about life were changed by a run of (seemingly unfounded) bad luck. Just the same, I've met people who've grown accustomed to living with repeated cycles of misfortune, believing that fate simply has it in for them.

Think back to the last time you had a run of bad luck. Maybe you woke up with a headache on an ordinary Monday morning and it persisted long after you took aspirin. The next day your car broke down and later you had an argument with a coworker. Then you lost your keys. To top it all off, you tripped on your way home. It sounds like an exaggeration, but we've all had those freaky experiences that make us throw up our hands and exclaim: "What's going on? I'm totally cursed!" A series of unfortunate events—even minor ones—deserves to be examined closely. Too often, however, we accept the challenges that disrupt our well-being and chalk them up to life's inevitable unfairness.

But is it really logical to assume that misfortune is random, that it manifests even after we've taken careful steps to ensure our success, our livelihood, our very safety? Don't get me wrong—sometimes setbacks occur, the best-laid plans crumble, and bad things happen to good people. But these aphorisms have become both our psychological imprints and our default reactions to what cannot be readily explained. As a society, we've been taught to view our personal hardships from the sidelines, standing by like helpless victims of circumstance. You were dealt bad cards and now you have to wait for the nastiness to dissipate. That's just the way it is. Sound familiar?

Back to the bad luck you encountered. Did you explain it away as "God's will" and then force yourself to push through it? Did you feel like there was a bull's eye on your back? Once it finally passed out of your life, did you live in fear that it would

The Evil Eye

waltz back in again? Your willingness to perceive bad luck as a random, invincible force is entirely normal. After all, these mental patterns have been hammered into our brains. When we label the occult "pseudoscience" or dismiss strange phenomena altogether, we're not only *accepting* the bad stuff that happens—we're *permitting* it and even opening up doors to more of it.

If we took the time to investigate the events that preceded a cycle of misfortune, we would (in most cases) see that cycle's point of origin. Yes: sometimes there *is* a concrete reason behind the sudden ailment, the mounting troubles in your career, the ongoing discord among family members. It's the Evil Eye at work. How did it enter your life? Perhaps you ran in to a former friend with whom you had a falling out months earlier, or you attended a family dinner and ended up sitting next to that cousin who's never liked you. Maybe it wasn't even as personal as the previous two examples, and you simply got into a spat with a stranger while waiting on line at the grocery store.

None of those people wished you well at the time. Their feelings of resentment, envy, or anger were projected on to you by way of an intentionally harmful look, and shortly thereafter your life took a disturbing turn. Logic might try to intervene here, but intuitively—and nothing is stronger than your intuition—you know that what happened to you or a loved one was too intense to rationalize or ignore.

Fortunately, you don't have to do either. The first step in combating the Evil Eye is being able to confirm its presence. Before we get to that list, I want to briefly clarify the difference between a symptom and a sign when it comes to the Evil Eye.

- A symptom is something you alone can see or recognize—it's subjective.

- A sign is evident to both you and others as an outward manifestation of a condition—it's objective.

If someone notices that you're behaving oddly or points out that you've been having bad luck, take the observation seriously because they might be seeing what you're unwilling to admit. When it comes to the Eye, it doesn't matter who points out what's happening. What matters is that the occurrence is identified and addressed.

One of the most common ways to diagnose the Evil Eye is the oil-and-water method. This entails filling a bowl with water, reciting a specific prayer, and then dropping olive oil into the bowl. If one or all of the drops disappear, the Eye is present. If the drops immediately start to spread and conjoin, the Eye is present. But if the drops of oil remain intact and simply float on the surface of the water, remaining entirely visible, the Eye is not present.

A common misconception is that the water-and-oil method is the only way to detect the Eye. This is false—as you will see in the forthcoming pages—and so is the notion that certain telltale shapes *always* appear on the surface of the water when the Evil Eye is present. Again, it depends on tradition and culture, but the presence of a particular shape isn't necessary in order to know that someone or something is under the quiet curse.

The Evil Eye can manifest in numerous ways, and the following lists explore how it can strike the body (physical or psychological manifestation) as well as one's surroundings (nonphysical manifestation). Please keep in mind that any ailment, pain, or trauma should always receive the attention of a health-care professional; if your doctor gives you a clean bill of health but the symptoms persist, the list below may prove particularly helpful. It's also important to remember that there are numerous conditions (like PTSD and generalized anxiety disorder [GAD], to name only a couple) that often produce physical and psychological symptoms—in some cases, the identical symptoms brought on by the Evil Eye. Do not discount any such conditions or automatically assume that the symptoms aren't because of acute onset of illness.

Whether you think you're in the grip of an Evil Eye or a loved one is, just remember to keep your mind open and your heart honest about the circumstances. In changing a negative condition, you're changing a life.

PHYSICAL OR CORPOREAL MANIFESTATIONS OF THE EVIL EYE

Bruising: that black-and-blue on your forearm is likely the result of having bumped into something (even if you don't remember doing so), but random bruises are cause for alarm; if this is the case, pay close attention to the shapes of the bruises— are they almond-shaped (like eyes) or do they have points (like horns)?

Dark circles: pigmentation changes as we age, but those pesky dark circles under the eyes don't just appear overnight; if they do, they are a symptom and a sign.

Eye twitch: it feels more like a spasm, or as if your eyelids are vibrating; the sensation lasts for a minute or two. It's believed in many Italian folk traditions that the left eye refers to a male and the right eye to a female, which might give you a clue about who could be responsible for casting the curse.

Falling: injuries and physical traumas happen, but if you take two or more bad falls in a matter of days and have no prior history of vertigo or a medical condition that causes dizziness or imbalance, it's not likely that you've suddenly become a klutz.

Hair loss: this is one of the extremely scary symptoms that manifests when the Evil Eye is a long term condition; much more severe than pattern baldness or a receding hairline, instead hair comes out in clumps.

Headache: it comes on suddenly and usually strikes the front of the head and the temples, and it will persist even after medication is ingested.

Hot or cold flashes: these come on quickly and intensely and usually strike the face and extremities. A man should be especially concerned if he feels a sudden rush of heat or coldness in his groin; the same is true when a woman feels a flash of heat or coldness in her breasts—these are signs of the Evil Eye targeting fertility.

Impotence: this is a symptom few men want to discuss, but it's extremely common. Sometimes relationships are a battleground. When discord ensues between lovers, you can be sure that ill intentions will be directed at the very part of the body many men value most.

Infertility: in many cultures there is a strong link between infertility and the Evil Eye, but the Eye doesn't relate solely to the inability to conceive. Miscarriages and ectopic pregnancies are often believed to be the result of jealousy, resentment, or too much talking/sharing about one's hopes to conceive.

Insomnia: occasional trouble sleeping is *not* synonymous with the inability to sleep. This is a symptom when you spend a night (or several nights) awake, sitting on the edge of your bed, wondering why your body just won't relax as it usually does.

Itching: this refers to the need to scratch a particular area of your body incessantly even when there's no sign of an insect bite, hive, or rash.

Leg cramps: the legs represent our ability to remain balanced and to move forward in life, so cramps are a sign that someone is jealous or angry about the advancements you're making.

Lethargy: a common condition experienced by everyone from time to time and for various reasons, but if it comes on abruptly, it should raise your suspicion. When you fall victim to the Eye, lethargy means that your energy is being drained away psychically.

Loss of appetite: again, this comes on suddenly and will be extremely pronounced. Take note—this is not the same as an "upset" stomach, indigestion, or the inability to keep food down; it's the absence of the desire to eat. While intermittent fasting or occasionally skipping a meal is normal for some people, a sudden loss of appetite is not. If you had a hearty breakfast and then feel inexplicably unable to eat lunch and dinner, the Eye might be at work.

Nose bleed: it's usually preceded by dryness in the nasal passages or irritation following a cold or infection. But when blood comes gushing out of one's nostrils unexpectedly, take heed.

Pallor: if you've ever walked into a room and been met with the "You look pale" comment, you're familiar with this sign. Be especially suspicious if pallor comes on suddenly.

Sleep paralysis: this is another severe symptom of the Eye and is sometimes accompanied by visual or auditory hallucinations.

Sneezing: allergies and dust can make you sneeze, but this is a sudden rush of sneezing that stops for several hours and then starts up again (without other accompanying symptoms of a cold or allergy irritation). Why? The nose is believed to be linked to personal power, be it in business or otherwise, and a powerful person is a sure target for envy.

Sore throat: when the throat is dry or in pain and infection has been ruled out, it's a good indication that your ability to communicate is under attack.

Sweating: this is a symptom when you know it's straight up odd for your forehead to be beaded in droplets. Is everyone else around you perfectly dry and comfortable? The Eye is almost always present if the back of your neck is damp while the rest of your body is dry.

Tearing: this is a sign when a speck of dust, an eyelash, or emotion can't be blamed for the tears streaking your face.

Teeth: another particularly frightening example of Evil Eye manifestation is of the dental variety; if a healthy tooth suddenly

cracks or falls out, don't be quick to dismiss it as solely a
medical problem.

Yawning: comes on suddenly, is usually excessive and
persistent; be especially suspicious if it's not accompanied
by lethargy.

PSYCHOLOGICAL MANIFESTATIONS
OF THE EVIL EYE

Aggression: it sounds straightforward, but every condition—be
it physical or psychological—is a bit more pronounced when
the Evil Eye is involved. Here, a person will feel unusually
aggressive toward the world *and* toward him/her/themselves.
The feeling can't be bottled up, so the afflicted individual
will lash out, often with uncharacteristic cruelty. The phrase
What's gotten into you? might sound suitable, but *What's been put
on you?* is really the right question to ask.

Anxiety: it sounds self-explanatory, but anxiety is a huge and
ugly beast with many tentacles. If you don't suffer from GAD
(generalized anxiety disorder) or aren't prone to occasional
anxiety, an unexplained bout of it may well be a result of
the Evil Eye. But before jumping to that conclusion, examine what's going on in your life at the time. Are you overly
stressed about something? When the Eye is to blame, anxiety
doesn't have an identifiable cause—it manifests in a steady
rush of negative thoughts about everything. A person will
fidget, pace, sigh continually, and be unable to hold a conversation for longer than a couple of minutes. The main
thought running through their head in a continuous loop is:
Why am I feeling this way?

Desperation: usually accompanied by intense anxiety or episodes of panic. A desperate person feels hopeless, like they're
willing to do anything to be rid of the dark emotion. If this

is your main symptom, examine where your mind is going. When the Eye is present, your thoughts will form a chain link of *what if?* scenarios.

Nightmares: while we've all had them, nightmares shouldn't be chronic. There are a host of reasons behind why you or a loved one is suffering from them (including nutritional factors), but a prolonged period of vivid nightmares is a common symptom of the Eye. If you don't remember your dreams, or aren't prone to nightmares but start having them, the Eye is likely at work.

Panic attacks: this symptom falls under the umbrella of anxiety, but panic attacks are also a specific beast; anyone who has had a panic attack knows that it is accompanied by a host of physical symptoms, among them accelerated heartbeat and hyperventilating. As above, it's necessary here to consider if there's a source to a panic attack. If a panic attack follows a negative confrontation, the Evil Eye is likely the cause, and further attacks will continue if the Eye is not removed.

Sadness: whether it hits you suddenly or grows little by little, the feeling is unmistakable —a heaviness that won't abate, a sense that life won't improve no matter what you do. Always ask yourself the most important question: Is there a concrete reason behind what I'm feeling? If not, the Eye is likely to blame.

Silence: this symptom isn't about not speaking; it refers, instead, to an unnatural and unfounded desire to withdraw from everyday life. Disinterest, indifference, a newly formed habit of shutting people and activities out of your life—they're all different ways of asking to be left alone. There's a huge line between contemplation and apathy; the former is a good thing, the latter is quite bad. If you or a loved one has descended into an apathetic place, it might be because some-one has stared you into it.

OTHER MANIFESTATIONS
OF THE EVIL EYE

As I noted earlier, the Evil Eye can infiltrate life in myriad ways. The mind and body take their hits, but the big picture of life has many moving parts. The following is a list of examples of how the quiet curse can make a lot of noise.

Bed sheets: The Evil Eye is insidious; it can start as a spark before the full blaze sets in, and this is one such example. If you live with your significant other and the two of you share a bed, pay special attention to the sheets. If a sheet rips while you're stripping or making the bed, or during sex, or after you or your partner tugs on it to get a little warmer, *don't* overlook it. The rip is an indication of the Eye working to disrupt your home environment, starting in the bedroom (which symbolizes love, intimacy, and trust).

Confusion in familiar environments: have you ever gotten into your car and settled in for a drive you've made two dozen times before only to get tripped up when you're on the highway? Or started on your regular jogging route but felt confused at a familiar bend in the road? It can be a terrifying experience that leaves you feeling disoriented, and it isn't always a sign of a neurological condition.

Dropping/losing items: plates, glasses, keys, other supplies . . . what at first presents itself as a funny kind of clumsiness can quickly become a nuisance. It's not normal to drop three plates in as many days, or to misplace things that make life run smoothly.

Fighting: it can be between you and your significant other, your kids, your best friend or coworkers or neighbors. The occasional argument is perfectly normal, but a stream of spats that has painted you as disagreeable and created palpable tension? Check the Evil Eye box.

Money: losing money suddenly or realizing that it's inexplicably going out faster than it's coming in may be a sign of the Eye. Financial issues and the Evil Eye are closely linked. Has a rush of problems created great expenses in your life? The refrigerator went on the blink? It happens to all of us from time to time, but when it's accompanied by car trouble, two traffic tickets, and an emergency dental procedure, the Eye is targeting your bank account.

Residential problems: the home—whether it's a studio apartment or a six-bedroom colonial—is a prime target for envy, and it's vital to recognize when a bad pattern is circulating through your abode. Did you just have a housewarming party? Did that friend who's always wanted to live in your city pay you a long visit? Burst pipes, leaks, and broken appliances are signs of the Eye. Have you ever had three light bulbs blow out within a very short period of time even when there's nothing wrong on the electrical front? Framed pictures sliding off of the walls? Again, a single incident isn't a big deal, but multiple mishaps need the kind of attention that the repairman likely can't provide.

Windows: yes, this might belong in the section about homes, but I've listed windows separately, as they hold specific significance: they are the "eyes" of a house. You can peer out of your windows unnoticed or just sit in front of one and observe the world beyond it. Unexplained cracks in the glass or frame of a window should be given close attention. If a window gets dirty or looks "caked" and filmy when it was clean a day or two earlier, it's a sign that all the individuals living in the house have been targeted. A suspicious crack in a child's bedroom window is an ominous sign of the Evil Eye.

SIGNS OF THE EVIL EYE IN NATURE

You might not be listening, but nature is always communicating with us. Some people call it universal wisdom, while others refer to it as the energy field. Many individuals believe they are surrounded by ancestral guides, angels, and animal spirits. The descriptions don't really matter: life just works better when we are attuned to the natural rhythms of the earth. Why? Because the earth is alive, and all we must do is be present and open to receiving the messages she sends us. As our world has become increasingly frantic and technological, many people have lost the ability to notice even the subtlest of signs unless something appears on Instagram or Facebook.

There are numerous ways to ward against the Evil Eye, but sometimes amulets aren't enough to keep it at bay; in these instances, it's wise to be aware of things that catch your eye—oddities in your immediate surroundings that give you pause. These oddities, disturbing though they may be, are often harbingers of foul energy in your midst, and recognizing them can help minimize or completely stop the Eye in its tracks.

Birds: magnificent creatures, birds can also be omens of negative energy flying toward you, and it's a bad sign if a bird pecks on a window of your home or car. A dead bird on a windowsill is also an omen of the Eye.

Carcasses: if you come upon more than one dead animal in a day—whether it's a field mouse or a moose—the Eye is "on your path."

Dead fish: if you live near a body of water and come upon a school of dead fish, make note of it; a single fish isn't unusual, but several of them are cause for alarm, even though there may also be other causes, such as toxic materials in the water.

Food: bloody eggs or fruits that rot quickly are considered bad omens. Finding worms in your food (not invisible parasites) is also indicative of the Eye.

Funerals: if you find yourself suddenly driving behind a funeral procession, or if you see a hearse more than once in a day, be particularly vigilant in figuring out whether or not the Eye is at work.

Different cultures, religions, and even locations recognize different signs, symptoms, and manifestations of the Evil Eye, so no list can be exhaustive or 100% definitive. Even so, the lists within this book demonstrate that the Eye is often the source of many problems—both short-term and those that persist until they become an accepted, integral part of a person's life. Have you ever met someone who says: "The lottery? Love at first sight? Those kinds of things don't happen to me." Then there are those who, in the midst of strange occurrences or sudden malaise, shrug their shoulders and say: "It's just my luck." It's more likely that an Evil Eye has created the condition.

Of course, the Eye isn't always the culprit. An accurate and effective practitioner has to be circumspect about these matters. There's a fine line between fanaticism and devotion, and the more you practice diagnosing and removing the Evil Eye, the more fine-tuned your senses will become.

Whenever someone asks me if they "have it," I always respond by posing a few simple questions before reaching for the olive oil. Here's a quick example:

- What are your symptoms? (What is your chief complaint?) For example, if my friend Jane tells me she has a headache and feels "off" or lethargic, I'll mentally log that as a physical symptom—but of what? That leads to my next question.

- When did you last eat or drink something? If Jane's response is "Six hours ago" or "I haven't eaten today," her symptoms may be the result of low blood sugar or dehydration, not the Eye. In this case, I would suggest that she eat and drink something immediately. If the symptoms persist an hour or two later, I'll do a diagnostic ritual.

Sometimes, symptoms aren't physical and may present ambiguously. For example, a couple of years ago, a friend called me and told me that the Eye was making his life a mess. I asked him to describe the "mess" and he quickly spouted off a list of psychological symptoms: he was moody, sad, annoyed, and everyone was angering him. That's not his general disposition. But then I remembered something important.

It was January, which in general isn't an easy time for my friend. Three years earlier, he and his ex-wife had gone through the worst of their divorce during January; his favorite uncle had also died in January. When I gently suggested that his symptoms might be related to a bit of residual trauma, my friend fell silent. After nearly a minute he said: "I hadn't thought of that. I really do hate this time of year." I texted him the next day and he informed me that nearly all of his symptoms had dissipated.

With time and experience, you will learn how to recognize these distinctions. Ironically, your own eyes will become sharper as you work to identify and remove the Evil Eye from those it has afflicted. But don't let the investigative part of the process consume you. The truth of the matter is that we can see quite plainly if a person is feeling unwell or behaving irrationally, just as we can discern when a person's bad luck is much more than their flat tire or lost wallet. Yes, there will always be that one friend or family member who's going to call you every time they get a headache, but in the main, people who believe they're suffering from the

The Evil Eye

effects of the Evil Eye are sincere in their assumptions. It's been my experience that performing a diagnosing ritual—regardless of the outcome—always helps.

BEFORE YOU BEGIN

If this is your first attempt at trying to diagnose the Evil Eye, it's important that you take a moment to ground and center yourself. Stop whatever you're doing. Sit in a quiet corner of your home or stand at a window and gaze up at the sky. Ten minutes of contemplation is sufficient, so long as you feel your head begin to clear. You can do a breathing exercise, or recite a prayer from whichever spiritual tradition comforts you.

The point of this simple grounding exercise is to get you to a place of stillness. Even thirty seconds of mental quiet will give you the fortitude to focus on the significance of the step you're about to take. The Evil Eye is an ancient and incredibly potent energy, not to mention the most insidious. Before you officially start, make sure you feel well on every front: physically, emotionally, and psychologically. The best way of ensuring your own spiritual fitness is to ask yourself the following questions:

Why do I want to learn to practice this kind of magic? Will it be a springboard for further study? Will you add to it so that it becomes a tradition you can pass on to your own children, nieces or nephews, grandchildren? Are you learning solely for the purpose of healing and protecting yourself and others? There's no wrong answer and asking these questions will make your own journey into this aspect of magic much clearer.

Am I ready to assume the responsibility that comes with it? You will undoubtedly become the "go-to" person in your family for all matters related to the Eye, and you can't pick and choose whom you want to perform the rituals for. You might well have to remove the Evil Eye for a person you don't always get along with. Be sure you're ready to accept that.

If your answers are motivated by curiosity or the desire to be the "powerful witch" in the family, much of what you're about to attempt will lead to disillusionment. This type of folk magic is about healing and protection, and you must have a sincere desire to do the work of a practitioner.

SELF-BLESSING OF THE HANDS

Your hands are the instruments that will guide you in diagnosing and banishing the Evil Eye. Gently mixing herbs, using your fingertips to drip the oil into the water, anointing a child's forehead—your hands do much of the sacred work. It's only appropriate that you bless each hand before you begin. Here is a simple but highly effective blessing:

Pour a tablespoon of olive oil into a small cup or a shot glass. Place a single clove into the olive oil. Let this sit for five minutes. Then, when you're ready, dip the thumb of your right hand into the oil and trace over the front and back of your left hand any symbol that represents your spiritual path, be it a cross, a Star of David, a pentacle, a dharma wheel, or anything else. If you don't have a connection to any spiritual path, simply dab your hand with the oil. As you do so, say the following: *That my fingers may bless. That my palms may heal. That my hands may protect.*

Repeat the process, using the thumb of your left hand to anoint your right hand. You can end with a prayer of your choosing, or by reciting meaningful verses. I happen to like Psalm 45:7: *Thou lovest righteousness, and hatest wickedness: therefore God, thy God, hath anointed thee with the oil of gladness above thy fellows.* Passages from the Quran and the sacred texts of Buddhism and Hinduism are equally powerful, as is the Charge of the Goddess. This ritual only has to be done once; there is no need to repeat it before doing any other rituals or spells.

METHODS TO DIAGNOSE
THE EVIL EYE

In Italian folk magic, the most common method to detect the Evil Eye is through oil and water. The origins of this particular tradition remain a mystery, but in Italy, the overwhelming majority of folk magic practitioners will tell you that the ritual has been a part of their family legacy for generations. I don't know when it started it my own family. I only know that it remains a significant part of my life and the lives of the people in my family and community.

But why oil and water? Like so many, I have often wondered about its origins. What do we know about the roots of this ritual? In a 2021 article I wrote about the Evil Eye, I posed that very question to Dr. Sabina Magliocco, a sociocultural anthropologist and leading authority on folklore and folk customs.

It is very difficult to find evidence of the roots of practices to cure or remove the evil eye, because these practices were passed down through oral tradition and imitation for centuries by ordinary people who were usually non-literate," Magliocco explained. "It is very likely, though, that practices such as using water and oil to diagnose and cure the evil eye predate Christianity, and that the prayers to saints for a cure were added when Christianity became the dominant religion. Certainly, the use of eye-shaped amulets to prevent the evil eye dates back to ancient Egyptian civilization, and therefore has pagan roots. It's worth noting, however, that often, practices with pagan roots combine with practices from monotheistic religions (Judaism, Christianity, Islam) in the prevention and cure of the evil eye.

Why, specifically, did our ancestors use water for this practice? They surely used other liquids and materials for divinatory purposes, but the water-and-oil method has survived the test of time.

When mixed, water and oil form two separate layers. According to science, oil should float on top of water because oil molecules stick together. But that's not always the case. As you'll soon discover, oil and water behave differently when practitioners use prayers, incantations, and intention to diagnose the Evil Eye.

What's the secret behind this phenomenon? How could such a simple method defy the laws of science? There are no definitive answers—that's precisely what makes it a mystery tradition. But those of us who practice these ancient rituals never doubt their efficacy. The prayers and secret incantations our ancestors whispered have survived over centuries and across bloodlines, proving that in the simplest words and actions we often find the strongest magic.

If you're new to folk magic and didn't have parents or grandparents who practiced the old ways, don't feel the least bit discouraged. In fact, you should feel just as empowered as those of us who inherited these traditions. Why? Because in learning how to diagnose and remove the Evil Eye, you are beginning your own tradition, claiming a key to enchantment that you will eventually pass on to your loved ones.

Before you take the next step, I want to explain the difference between diagnosing the Evil Eye and curing it. There are many practitioners who believe that once the Eye is detected—be it in a bowl of water or another method—it can be eradicated with a handful of salt or a pair of scissors. Sprinkle, jab, cut. . . the Eye bursts and relieves the afflicted individual's symptoms. Simple and fast. Cut and dry. I also believe this is true—but only to a certain extent.

It's been my experience that there are different degrees of Evil Eye energy. Sometimes it manifests as a headache or lethargy. Sometimes it's a day of minor unfortunate events. But the majority of Evil Eye manifestations wreak havoc on a grand scale: emotionally, psychologically, and physically. These are the cases where relationships deteriorate, family members fight and grow apart, houses crumble. These are the cases where the body breaks down and infertility, impotency, and other ailments persist. These are the cases where jobs are lost, bank accounts dry up, and deep despair sets in.

When the Eye is that strong—and most of the time, it is—practitioners need stronger magic to banish it. And that's exactly what you'll find in the next chapter: a plethora of detailed spells and rituals for those instances when ridding yourself or someone else of the Evil Eye calls for more than salt, scissors, a knife, or an incantation. Ultimately, it will be up to you, the practitioner, to decide what kind of magical action to take and which spells to perform.

If you find yourself dealing with what seems like a minor case with minor symptoms, a simple blessing or benediction may clear things up. But if an expectant mother is having trouble or a child appears to have fallen victim to the Eye, you'll have to up your magical ante and choose a spell that's going to fix the negative condition. Spells and rituals may be found in chapter 5, starting on page 153.

Read through the following methods. Ask yourself which one "feels" right for you. Some of us are comfortable with simple rituals that get the job done quickly. Some of us—I might be raising my hand here—prefer more elaborate rituals that require time and make our kitchen counters look like occult shops. Every one of the following methods is valid and will grant you the ability to diagnose the Eye. You can experiment with all of them, but ultimately it's best to choose one method and make it your own. Practice it, meditate on it, and use it until it becomes second nature.

What you will find here are several methods to diagnose the Evil Eye. I was raised in a Catholic home where folk magic was common, so I'm quite familiar with malocchio, saint magic, Christological terminology, and all things Italian. The years I've spent studying and practicing magic have enriched my life and broadened my scope of knowledge as a folk witch. Folk magic draws from numerous cultures and traditions, a rich tapestry that transcends the boundaries of doctrine and dogma. That's why the methods you'll find here also come from Hindu, Jewish, Muslim, and Zoroastrian traditions, among others. I have arranged the methods alphabetically according to the names I've given them; where applicable, I have also identified their religious or cultural origin. Inclusivity is important when it comes to magic and ritual. The spiritual path is about learning new ways of thinking, praying, meditating, and healing, but it's also about being empowered through our manifold oneness.

For the methods that require oil and water, you always will need the following:

- A bowl of water

- A bottle of olive oil

- A spoon

How to make your diagnosis: After filling the spoon with olive oil, gently dip your index finger into the oil so that a film of it gathers on your fingertip. You will recite a specific prayer or incantation depending upon which method you choose to use. Let the oil fall from your fingertip into the bowl. Then look closely at the water.

- If the drops begin to move toward each other or grow—especially if any assume an ocular shape—the Evil Eye is present.

- If the drops completely vanish after they've hit the water, it's also a sign that the Eye is present.

- If the drops simply stay in place and do what oil is *supposed* to do in water, then the Eye is *not* present.

One more important note: *always* fill your bowl or dish of water quietly, without speaking to anyone else; silent water has healing properties.

By Scent (Hindu)

Gather the following items and place them in a piece of parchment or cloth:

- Two red chili peppers

- Seven mustard seeds

- A pinch of salt

Fold the peppers, seeds and salt into the paper or cloth to form a packet or pouch. Circle the pouch, clockwise, around the afflicted individual's head seven times. The following step requires the packet, or its ingredients, to be burned, but if you want to conserve the paper or cloth, empty the ingredients into a pot or fireproof container and burn them. Otherwise, toss the entire packet into a fire.

What do you smell? If the scent if highly or unusually acrid (sometimes causing one's eyes to water or burn), the Eye is present. If the scent is tolerable, the Eye is not present.

The Christmas Eve Malocchio Ritual

The handing down of the malocchio prayer is an old tradition, and while no one can pinpoint when it started, it is deeply rooted in Italian-American culture. Why Christmas Eve? No one knows for certain, but the birth of Jesus Christ symbolizes light—a luminescence that awakens knowledge and brings about hope and healing. But as I wrote earlier, this is not *strictly* done on Christmas Eve. When and how the prayer and ritual are passed down is up to the elder or individual who possesses the knowledge. Some bestow it on a particular Catholic feast day (generally one commemorating a saint or the Virgin Mary); others choose a day that has meaning for their own family, like an ancestor's birthday or date of death.

In many Italian homes, December 24th is more festive than Christmas Day itself. On Christmas Eve, families traditionally gather to share the "seven fishes" meal, exchange gifts, and attend midnight Mass. If you're the chosen recipient of the malocchio prayer, you'll have work to do before heading off to church with your siblings and cousins.

In placing this ritual here, I am not "handing it down" to you. I am including it so that you can begin your own tradition. This means you accept the responsibility that comes with knowing how to diagnose and cure malocchio, as well as the responsibility of making sure you pass the ritual on. Magic is strengthened through customs that are carried forward.

Does this mean you have to be Italian or Italian-American to learn and pass the ritual on? Of course not. A tradition is created the moment someone decides that a particular practice will *become* a tradition. You claim it, name it, and frame it so that it forms a permanent portrait in your soul. My grandmother didn't know when the malocchio ritual began in her lineage, for example, but that didn't matter to her. Nor does it matter to my aunt and sister, who represent an unbroken chain of female practitioners in my family.

While this is an old ritual rooted in the folk Catholic tradition, keep in mind that the only requirement for learning it and practicing it is the honest desire to do so. Your sex, age, gender identity, spiritual beliefs, or any other matters related to your identity don't matter.

Here are the ritual and prayers. Remember that Italian folk magic is an oral tradition, so these prayers are not handed down in written form; they are spoken in the dialect of a particular region.

A couple of points to keep in mind: On Christmas Eve, make sure to set aside time for yourself, as you will need to be alone. The ritual is generally done in the kitchen, but if there's another room you wish to use, by all means do so. Gather the following ingredients beforehand and set them aside in a safe place:

- A bowl

- A spoon

- Olive oil

- A sprig of rue or rosemary, or one bay leaf

- A handkerchief

- An image of Jesus Christ (though not an image of the crucifixion); a laminated holy card works best

When you are alone and ready, stand before the items and spend at least a full minute in silence. Then follow these steps: Fill the bowl with water. Make the sign of the cross. Place the fingertips of your dominant hand on the edge of the bowl closest to you and recite one "Our Father," one "Hail Mary," and one "Glory Be" prayer.

Fill the spoon with olive oil. Dip the index finger of your dominant hand into the oil, and as you let one drop fall into the bowl, say: *I take the sword.* Dip your finger into the oil a second time, and as you let a second drop fall into the bowl, say: *I take the shield.* Dip your finger into the oil a third time, and as you let a third drop fall into the bowl, say: *Holding both, I am healed.*

If there's any olive oil left on the spoon, pour it into the bowl and then set the spoon aside. Don't mind what happens in the water. Pick up either the sprig of rosemary or rue, or the bay leaf, and dip it into the water, making sure it is completely submerged, then quickly take it out and set the sprig or leaf on the handkerchief.

Now recite one of the following prayers out loud; read each one first and decide whether you prefer the Italian one or the English one.

In Italian:
Uno ha pensato
Due ti hanno guardato
Tre e si ammalato
Con l'aiuto della Madonna e Gesu Cristo
Mando via quest'occhio triste!

In English:
One thought of you
Two looked at you
Three and you're sick.
With the help of the Blessed Mother and Jesus Christ
I send away this sad eye!

Here, you are going to add the name of an ancestor you wish to honor and invoke. This can be any loved one who has passed over. It doesn't matter if you knew the individual personally or if you know stories about them—it's the essence of who they were in life that you are calling forth. Speak the person's name three times. This is what makes the prayer your own. When you pass the prayer on with your additions, it is now a secret tradition.

As you can see, the prayer rhymes in Italian, which makes it easier to remember. The first line of the prayer refers to the person who had envious or negative thoughts about you. The second line refers to that person's eyes looking at you. The third line (and the number three) refers to a sickness that is of mind, body, and spirit.

This is a second prayer I was taught, which I have written out phonetically in dialect:

E 'minnuta cu doya
So meesa dentra l'oil
Shciatt' l'invidia
E creppa ru'malocchio
Sant'Antonio e San Michele
Aqua, sole, e purra ru'stelle!

If you choose to use this prayer, add the name of your ancestor at the end just as you did above.

A more recent prayer, short but powerful, calls on Padre Pio:

Padre Pio
Hold my hands
Stand with me
As evil disbands.

After you have selected a prayer and memorized it, pour the water down the drain and wash the bowl and spoon. Gently place the holy card over the bay leaf, or the sprig of rue or rosemary and carefully wrap it all up with the handkerchief.

The last of the ritual happens in church, so you will have to attend Midnight Mass. Try to get a seat close to the chancel; if that's not possible, make sure you at least have a clear view of the altar. Pay close attention as the priest raises the Eucharist. Lock eyes with the moment of transubstantiation. As the priest says the words "This is the body and blood of Christ," touch the handkerchief containing the card and your selected herb with your dominant hand.

Later, preferably when the Mass has ended and while people are filing out of the church, go to an icon at which people pray and discreetly leave the bay leaf/sprig of rue or rosemary there. With this gesture, you are making an offering of thanks and a promise to use the prayers fairly and wisely.

Keep the holy card with you—in your wallet or purse—or put it in a private place.

Use the same ritual when you are ready to pass down your chosen prayer to a trusted friend or member of your family. This might be one year later or it might be twenty years later, but it should be done on Christmas Eve.

Dropping the Crumbs

This method is quick and easy and requires only two items: a glass or bottle of water (it can be a regular plastic bottle) and a piece of bread.

Place the glass or bottle of water in front of you. Pinch three crumbs from a piece of bread and rest them on a clean napkin or sheet of paper. Make sure not to roll the pieces into tiny balls or flatten them between your thumb and forefinger. Holding one hand over the glass of water and the other over the bread, chant the following incantation, which is a rough translation of a *scongiuro* (charm) originally handed down to me in Neapolitan dialect: *Water strong and water deep, bread for the body that I keep, every day and every week, as I wake and as I sleep.*

Place the crumbs in the palm of your dominant hand, and then drop them, individually but in rapid succession, into the glass. If only one crumb sinks, the Evil Eye is not present. If two or more sink, the Eye is at work.

The Egg Test (Morocco)

The following ritual was told to me by an individual from Morocco whom I interviewed in the spring of 2022. Take an egg and carefully and slowly hold it over the afflicted individual's outstretched hands, keeping certain they hold their palms up. After a few seconds, make an X in three consecutives motions over their palms.

Crack the egg into a bowl and study the yolk. If the yolk is split or doubled, the Eye is present. Similarly, if there are bubbles in the yolk, the Eye is present and the envy is being transmitted by a close relation.

The Elemental Eye (Pagan)

There's nothing more natural than calling on the elements of earth, air, fire, and water. While common in many pagan rituals, the practice isn't strictly related to witchcraft or shamanism. An average of 60% of the human body is comprised of water, and life itself wouldn't exist without the forces of air, fire, and earth. Those who wish to work without specific religious connotations may feel more comfortable using this method to diagnose the Evil Eye.

Gather the following items and ingredients:

- A bowl of water

- A spoon

- Olive oil

- Two bay leaves

Fill the bowl with water and set it on a firm surface, making sure the spoon and olive oil are in easy reach. Pick up the bay leaves and, cupping them in both of your palms, bring them close to your lips and blow on them. Then set them down on either side of the bowl.

Moisten your right thumb with your saliva and then anoint your right eyelid. Repeat with your left thumb and left eyelid. Using the thumb of your dominant hand, you're now going to anoint the bowl in a clockwise manner, starting at the top (north/earth) and ending on the left side of the bowl (water/west). As you touch north, say: *"By earth it's exposed."* Touching east, say: *"By air it's revealed."* Touching south, say: *"By fire, it's seen."* Touching west, say: *"By water, it's divined."*

If you feel a flash of heat in your hands or a gentle bristle of wind around you, don't be alarmed. You're working with the natural powers of the universe, and those powers are responding.

Pick up the spoon and olive oil and follow the steps noted on page 132 to make your diagnosis. If the Eye is present, neutralize the energy by dropping the bay leaves into the bowl.

The Holy Trinity (Catholic/Christian)

Gather the following items:

- A bowl of water

- Olive oil

- A spoon

- A pinch of salt

First, make the sign of the cross. Now make the sign of the cross over the bowl, touching each point with your index and middle fingers: top (Father), bottom (Son), left side (Holy), right side (Spirit). Say aloud the name of the person or persons for whom the ritual is being performed. "For John," or "For Steve and Carol." You can also diagnose for a house, a car, a new project. Just be specific and name it. If you can't speak aloud, inwardly say the name of the person or object. Recite the following: *God in His might defends. Christ in His mercy amends. And all evil the Holy Spirit ends.*

Pick up the spoon and gently pour some olive oil into it. Dip your index finger into the oil and, holding it over the bowl, let two or three drops fall into the water, not on top of each other but in different parts of the bowl. Make certain not to spill whatever oil is left in the spoon; carefully pour it back into the bottle.

Now look down into the bowl. What do you see when the Eye is clearly present? Add a pinch of salt to the water; this neutralizes the negativity, but it does *not* banish the harm. (Remember: diagnosing the Evil Eye and removing it are two different things. In the next chapter you'll find many spells, rituals, and prayers for banishing it.) After adding the pinch of salt, you can dump the water out, preferably outside of your home, but if that's not an option, pouring it down a drain is fine.

Matched Up

Another simple way to diagnose the Evil Eye utilizes matches and water. I prefer a box of matches, but a book of matches will work as well. You will also need a bowl or large cup of water.

An incantation isn't necessary here, but before you begin, it's important that you center yourself and bring to mind the person or persons for whom you are diagnosing the Eye. If it's about a house, a car, a new job, or any other particular situation, concentrate on it as you gather three matches into the palm of your dominant hand. Close your eyes and focus on the matter. When you feel ready, open your eyes, light the first match and, while staring at the flame, quietly speak the person's name or the situation for which you're doing the working. Then toss the match into the bowl of water. Quickly light the other two matches and toss them into the bowl as well. Let a full three minutes pass. Look into the bowl again and study the matches.

- If they have migrated towards each other in a clump—especially if two of them have crossed and formed an X—then the Evil Eye is present.

- If all three matches have sunk to the bottom of the bowl, the Eye is present.

- If the matches are far apart or stuck to the sides of the bowl, the Eye is *not* present.

Mother Mary (Catholic)

The Sub Tuum Praesidium prayer is believed to be the oldest known prayer to the Virgin Mary. Dating back to c. 300 CE, it is known in the Catholic Church as well as the Eastern Orthodox Church. The prayer is especially effective when diagnosing the Evil Eye for children and expectant mothers.

Begin in the usual manner. Make the sign of the cross, and then make it over the bowl. After filling the spoon with oil, recite the prayer:

We turn to thy protection, O Holy Mother of God. Listen to our prayers and assist us in our needs. Deliver us from every danger, glorious and blessed Virgin.

Add the drops of oil into the water and make your diagnosis.

Name the Egg (Turkey)

The practice of *oomancy*—divination by eggs—is as old as it is common. There are numerous methods to read an egg, depending on one's culture, religion, and even one's personal beliefs. Saba, a Muslim woman I interviewed about Islam and the Evil Eye, shared the following method with me. Saba believes profoundly in the Evil Eye and practices various rituals to diagnose, remove, and ward it off in the privacy of her own home. She doesn't know where the egg method originated; it was given to her by an older relative two decades ago, and Saba has used it with complete success ever since.

You will need the following:

• One egg

• A pencil

• A sock

• A coin or pebble

• A sheet of paper

There are no prayers or incantations to recite. If someone suspects they have the Evil Eye, or if you suspect the Eye is present, try this method of diagnosis, which can be performed anywhere.

Start by asking the person who believes they're afflicted with the Eye about the events of their day. Ask them to pay special attention to the people with whom they were in contact— they don't have to narrow it down to *every* person, but they should be able to home in on any interactions or instances that felt "off" or strained or just plain odd. Did a coworker criticize them? Did a stranger on the train compliment their hair or eyes? Did they boast about their new house?

The point is to narrow down the list to a few names. Write the names on the sheet of paper with the pencil; you don't have to be letter-perfect, so if one of the people mentioned is "the crazy guy at the supermarket," write down "stranger/crazy guy." If diagnosing for yourself, the same instructions apply.

When the list is complete, hold the egg in your non-dominant hand. With your dominant hand, pick up the pencil and gently etch each name onto the eggshell. If the egg cracks while you're writing, dispose of it and start with a fresh one. When you've finished writing the names, slip the egg into the sock and tuck the coin or pebble in with it.

If the afflicted person is with you, have them sit on a chair. Standing over them, hold the sock up and swing it clockwise seven times, making seven circles above and around their head. Pause, and then repeat the process going counterclockwise. (If you're doing this ritual for yourself, follow the same instructions, making certain not to hit your own head.)

Gently remove the egg from the sock; if it begins to leak as you take it out, examine the shell closely. Find the most obvious crack or indentation and note which name is closest to it; it might even be directly over a name you etched onto the shell. If such is the case, the Evil Eye is present. Note that the Eye is present as long as there is a crack in the eggshell—it doesn't have to be leaking. If the egg remains intact, the Eye is *not* present.

If you've determined that the Eye is present, put the egg back into the sock (along with the coin), tie it up, and throw everything away, preferably in a river or stream. If you're not close to a body of water, bury it as far away from your home, or wherever you performed the ritual, as possible.

The point of this ritual is twofold: it detects the presence of the Evil Eye and also reveals the identity of the person who cast it. According to Saba, the curse is broken once the egg is disposed of because the egg absorbed the evil and its intention. The egg also provided you with clear answers about the situation, so you know to stay away from the person whose name was closest to the crack or indentation.

The Packet Ruqya (Islam)

Gather the following ingredients:

- A pinch of salt

- The peel of one onion

- Two or three nigella seeds

- A strand of the afflicted individual's hair (if the afflicted is a child, use a strand of their mother's hair)

Wrap the ingredients into a piece of paper or parchment and recite the following:

O, Allah! Lord of the people, the Remover of harm. Cure [recite the individual's name]! You are the One who cures. None brings about healing but You; a healing that will leave behind no ailment.

Throw the packet into a fire. If a popping sound is heard within the first minute, or if the flames burn unusually high, the Evil Eye is present.

The Power of Touch (Catholic/Christian)

The simplest method to detect if the Evil Eye is at work in someone's life or affairs is through your own hands. Here, a practitioner and the individual who suspects they are afflicted must stand face to face. The practitioner places the palm of their right hand against the forehead of the individual, just above the eyes.

Without looking into the individual's eyes, the practitioner recites the following incantation:

She looked to the skies while holding her eyes and God in is his might restored her sight. Saint Lucy in Heaven, grant us your vision, stand beside us, and reveal the condition.

If either the practitioner or the possibly afflicted individual yawns, or if their eyes begin to tear, the Evil Eye is present.

Tarot

Tarot cards are among the most favored form of divination. They are consulted for all matters of life: love, career, finances, and virtually anything you can think of, as well as just to get a general sense of what energy is unfolding in life at the current moment and where it might lead. But the tarot isn't *only* effective for divination. I have personally used the cards for spellwork, meditation, and, yes, to diagnose the Evil Eye.

Like most practitioners, you will likely become comfortable with diagnosing the Eye via the oil-and-water method. But what do you do when you're sitting on a bus or train and someone texts you with a request to diagnose? What if you're on vacation? You will undoubtedly find yourself sitting at your desk at work when that frantic call comes through. You probably won't have the necessary accoutrements at arm's reach. I'm a pretty hardcore folk witch, but I don't have a bottle of olive oil in my car, nor do I carry one in my briefcase or backpack. I do, however, have at least one deck of tarot cards with me whenever I leave home. I've been asked to diagnose the Eye while away from home more times than I count. I used to hate having to say, "I can't right now," or "I'll be able to do it later," to someone who isn't feeling well or is genuinely scared. Thankfully, that's no longer a problem because of the tarot. I highly recommend carrying a deck of tarot cards with you.

I was taught the following method several years ago by a wise old and wonderful mago (also called a magone) from Naples, Italy. Originally, he showed me how to look for 'na fattura (a curse) using Neapolitan playing cards. (If you're a child of Italian immigrants or had Italian grandparents, you've likely seen them gather around the table for a game of *Scopa* or *Briscola*.) It's a simple formula—so simple, in fact, that it almost looks like a game.

Remove the following cards from your tarot deck in the following order: Ten of Swords, Seven of Swords, The Devil, The Star, The Sun, Temperance. Place the six pulled cards one on top of the next, facedown. Take a few deep breaths. When you feel ready, pick up the six stacked cards and begin shuffling them. Remember to keep the cards facedown.

As you shuffle, chant the following incantation three times:

Archangel Michael sees what the devil hides, anger bursts and envy dies, and I now have the Archangel's eyes.

I recommend memorizing the incantation so that you can keep your eyes closed as you shuffle the cards; do this for at least a minute. When you feel ready to open your eyes, flip the top card of the stack over.

If the first card is the Seven of Swords, the Evil Eye is present and is the result of another's envy, deceit, or intent to harm.

If the first card is the Ten of Swords, the Eye is present and is the result of one's own boasting (whether consciously or obliviously). This serves as a warning to the afflicted that they should reexamine their behavior and speech about what and how they share details of their personal life.

If the first card is the Devil, the Eye is present and the direct result of another's manipulation. To be even clearer: when this card shows up first, the afflicted individual is being transmitted negativity not through an obvious, angry glance but via a sugar-coated stare that conceals envy and bad intentions. The offender is almost always a close relation. This isn't an easy message to convey to the afflicted, as it's telling them that someone they trust is silently betraying them. But it's the duty of a practitioner to be honest, and so convey the message you must.

If the first cards are The Sun, The Star, or Temperance, the Eye is not present.

Three Powers (Catholic)

This method is similar to the previous one, but it utilizes an Italian incantation. I was taught to perform this method by placing the bowl on top of the afflicted individual's head, so they should be seated in a chair close to where you are standing.

Begin by making the sign of the cross. Lift the bowl with both of your hands and then gently set it down on top of the person's head, certain that it's steady and won't fall and break. Make the sign of the cross over the bowl. Recite the following incantation, either to yourself or in a barely audible whisper:

Chiamo la Madonna e Jesu Christo. [Afflicted individual's name] e malato e tristo! Santa Rita, apri la porta. Cacchia chi m'guardato storta!

Translated: I call the Madonna and Jesus Christ. [Afflicted individual's name] is sick and sad. Saint Rita, open the door. Throw out the one who gave me a crooked stare!

Drop the olive oil into the bowl and make your diagnosis.

Triple Goddess (Pagan)

Three is a sacred number in many traditions. Numerologically, it represents balance. It also represents the goddess in her aspects of maiden, mother, and crone. Here, you will diagnose the Evil Eye using an invocation to the mother goddess. All that's needed is olive oil, a spoon, and a bowl of water.

Begin by anointing the rim of the bowl with a triangle, starting at the lower left point; as you trace a line with your index finger from here to the top of the bowl, say: "Mother." Move your index finger from the top point to the lower right side of the bowl, saying: "Maiden." From the lower right point, trace another line straight across to the first point on the lower left and say: "Crone."

Holding both hands above the bowl, recite the following incantation:

Great Mother Goddess of moon and sun, show me all that has been done. Here I stand at the liminal crossroads and invoke the One who always knows.

Drip olive oil into the bowl and make your diagnosis.

Two Prayers (Eastern Orthodox Christianity/Greek)

When it comes to the Evil Eye (mati) and its diagnosis and cure, Greek culture is deeply intertwined with Eastern Orthodox Christianity. Greeks do not always employ oil and water to diagnose mati. (When they do, it is usually not a bowl of water that is used, but a cup.)

To see if the Eye is present, a healer recites one of the following two prayers silently. This can be done in the presence of the afflicted individual or while the healer is alone. Immediately following the recitation, the healer should sit quietly for a few minutes, preferably alone. If the healer begins to yawn, or if their eyes begin to tear up, the Eye is present. (Both of the following prayers were given to me by a native of Greece, and he assisted in their translations so that they are as close as possible to the prayers that have been in his own family for generations.)

Prayer One:
Jesus Christ, He who conquers all and dispels all evil.
He casts all evil to the mountains, to the highest mountains
And deepest waters. Cure [insert the individual's name],
In the Name of the Father, the Son, and the Holy Spirit.

Prayer Two:
O Holy Virgin, Mother of God,
Look upon [name individual] with grace,
Touch your hands to (his/her/their) face
Take all envy and harm to your Divine Son

Water Touch Method

Gather the following ingredients:

- A bowl of water

- One sprig of rosemary

- A spoon

- Olive oil

Set the bowl of water on a counter or hard surface. The kitchen counter is probably best, since spilling may occur. Place the sprig of rosemary into the bowl. Instruct the afflicted individual to place their index and middle finger into the bowl. Fill the spoon with olive oil. Let a single drop fall into the bowl. If the drop remains visible, the Eye is not present. If the drop vanishes, the Eye is at work. In the latter case, remove the rosemary from the water and instruct the afflicted individual to bury it at sunset the next day.

WHO GAVE YOU THE EVIL EYE?

It's probably the second most popular question every practitioner of Evil Eye magic is asked: *"Who gave it to me?!"* While the curiosity is entirely understandable, there are no definitive methods to unmask the offender. The following methods, however, will offer up strong clues. A note of cautionary advice: If you do figure out who gave you or a loved one the Evil Eye, don't confront the envious party. Instead, refer to the selection of spells and rituals in the following chapter. Confrontation won't solve the problem. Magic will.

Divine the Shapes

This method uses olive oil, water, and salt to reveal the sex of the individual who gave the Evil Eye to either you or your loved one by invoking Marie Laveau and St. Anthony of Padua. This is one of my favorite rituals, as it calls upon Saint Anthony of Padua (my patron saint, and on whose feast day I was born) and Marie Laveau, to whom I have a strong devotion. Madame Marie also worked with Saint Anthony and asked for his assistance in many of her rituals. According to legend, if Saint Anthony didn't work quickly enough for her, she turned a statue of him upside down and left him "on his head" until he came through. I have found that calling on Saint Anthony and Madame Marie creates potent magic. When they join hands, a portal opens.

You will need the following:

• A bowl of water

• A teaspoon of olive oil

- A sprinkle of salt

- A knife

Place the bowl of water on a clean, firm surface. Sprinkle a pinch of salt into it. Then recite the following incantation:

Madame Marie, Madame Marie, take the hand of Saint Anthony and together reveal the secret to me.

Pour two drops of olive oil into the bowl. Pick up the knife and gently puncture each drop of olive oil once. Wait and watch the drops as they move. If a circle forms, the identity is that of a woman. If a line forms, the identity is that of the man. If a triangular shape forms, the identity is that of a nonbinary individual.

Pouring Lead: Blei Gissen

The practice of *blei gissen* ("pouring lead" in Yiddish) is the pouring of molten lead into a pot of cold water to both diagnose and treat the Evil Eye, or ayin hara. This method is not exclusively Jewish; in fact, it is practiced widely across Europe and parts of the Middle East. (The practice itself is officially called molybdomancy.)

While blei gissen is old—those who do it claim that it has roots in the Gemara, a component of the Talmud—it can also be dangerous, as lead is poisonous and it gets extremely hot. Included here is the basic ritual, but it is perfectly acceptable to use tin instead of lead. In fact, in Germany, kits are sold for this very purpose, containing only tin.

A few points to remember: It's best to do this outside to minimize the risk of poisoning and fire, but if you insist on doing it indoors, make certain your living space is very well ventilated. If you're pregnant or think you might be pregnant, don't do it. Pregnant individuals should not be in the immediate vicinity of melted lead or tin. Use a cast-iron skillet and an aluminum-slotted spoon, along with an aluminum ladle. (Don't use these accoutrements for any of kind of cooking afterward.) Use goggles and gloves made for wearing when melting metals. Dress for the part—long sleeves and pants only! Make sure your hair is tied back away from your face, or wear a hat or hairnet.

You will need:

- A cast-iron skillet

- A glass bowl filled with cold water

- A small bar of lead, or pellets of lead

- A quilt or heavy covering

- An aluminum-slotted spoon or ladle

Traditionally, the afflicted individual sits in a chair close to the stove; they are covered with a quilt or sheet and handed a *tefillah* (prayer) to read. The healer or caster should heat up a skillet and add the bar or pellets of lead. Pay close attention, as the lead will liquefy quickly. Once it does, use the ladle and scoop the liquefied lead from the pan and carefully pour some into the bowl of cold water. Transfer the bowl of water, holding it on top of the afflicted individual's head. The individual should continue reading the tefillah. (Use extreme caution when holding the bowl above the afflicted individual's head.) When they are finished reading, set the bowl down and remove the sheet from the individual's head.

Now study the formations in the water. It's likely that the lead has formed long sticklike shapes; some may be as short and thin as twigs. If you see spherical or circular shapes at the end of any of these sticks, you're seeing an Evil Eye.

Wax and Water

Known as carromancy, this form of divination utilizes two simple tools: a bowl of water and wax. It's simple and powerful, but not always fast. The effort, however, is worth the reward, as carromancy tends to yield startlingly accurate results.

You will need:

- One candle (I generally use a white or purple taper or chime candle)

- One candle holder

- A bowl of cold water (I never use a bowl that's the same color of the candle, as it tends to make reading the wax more difficult.)

- A lighter or matches

- A sprig of rue (this is optional, but it's how I was taught to do it)

There is debate about what kind of water should be used. Some say it should be spring water, others say it should be moon water (this is water that has been left on a windowsill or outside to absorb the energy of the full moon). Many believe the ritual works best if holy water is used. We don't always have access to a spring or a church to collect holy water, so in most cases I fill a bowl with water from the tap and then bless it myself. To do this, simply recite any prayer that empowers you. If prayer isn't your preference, speak your intention—to receive hidden information—directly into the water.

Next, pick up the candle and hold it so that it's against both of your palms. Hold the candle until you can feel your heartbeat pulsing against it.

The Evil Eye

After this, dip the sprig of rue into the water three times while speaking the name of the person or situation you are performing the ritual for (again, the rue is optional).

Light the candle and let it burn for a minute; turn it over gently and lower it so that it's close to the surface of the water. Let three drops of wax fall into the water. Now move the candle in a counterclockwise direction. Do this for several minutes, or until the bowl is teeming with hardened bits of wax. When you replace the candle to its holder, study the bowl again. Look at the shapes that have formed in the water.

What do you see? You might notice letters or numbers. You might see shapes that resemble flowers, airplanes, doors, a crescent moon. These are clues about the identity of the person or persons who is giving you the Evil Eye.

A friend did this ritual with remarkable results. He wanted to know who was harboring feelings of envy and resentment toward him, and just as he began studying the wax formations, he found among them a perfectly formed skeleton key and the numbers four and six; these were direct references to one of his coworkers, a woman who always wore a skeleton key pendant around her neck and whose birthday is June 4th. I've had people tell me that they've found initials, anniversary dates, even images of human profiles that were startlingly familiar.

Make note of your findings. Draw or take photos of them. Even if particular symbols don't make sense initially, something might click when you see them gathered together or arranged on a sheet of paper.

CHAPTER FIVE

HOW TO CURE THE EVIL EYE: SPELLS, PRAYERS, MAGIC, AND RITUALS

Many believe that the Evil Eye can only be banished in one of two ways: by a trained magical practitioner or by someone who has inherited a mysterious (and closely guarded) family ritual passed down through generations. While these theories remain prevalent in certain parts of the world and among certain cultures, the truth is far different. It is entirely possible for anyone to learn how to cure the Evil Eye.

You needn't be a witch, shaman, or occultist to master this ancient and sacred form of magic. You don't have to subscribe to a particular religion, either. That said, becoming adept at removing the Eye isn't as simple as choosing a technique and practicing it a few times until you feel comfortable with the process. It doesn't work that way. In fact, the *process* must feel comfortable with *you*.

Read that last sentence again. I'm purposely highlighting the word "process" here because removing the Evil Eye is both a craft and an art. It requires concentration, discipline, faith, patience, willpower, and courage. It's a skill you will learn and hone and keep for the rest of your life. Eventually, you may even tweak the rituals and spells in this book to fit your own personal beliefs and identity.

In the previous chapter, you learned how to diagnose the Evil Eye through a variety of methods. Now you're going to take the next step and come to know the various ways in which to remove and banish it. Before you start, it's imperative that you understand a few key points about the process.

First, you must have a sincere desire to both understand the process and accept the responsibility that comes with removing and banishing the Evil Eye. It's serious business, and you will be working both *with* energy and *against* energy. For example, if you choose to use the Saint Lucy Eye-Busting spell, the energy you invoke through the power of that saint will assist you in dispelling the negativity afflicting you or a loved one. It's a kind of battle-field. The negative energy dissipates because it changes form, and it changes form because your magic is stronger than *it*.

Second, be responsible. Learning to cure the Eye is a specific kind of folk magic; it is simultaneously a healing ritual, a protection ritual, *and* a banishing ritual. I think of it as a spiritual crossroads, and it works. You *must* remember your own self-care before you can successfully help someone else. If you're under the weather or wound up with anxiety, don't jump into a ritual or spell. Take some time to ground yourself, either through breathing exercises, or a quick walk outside. You can even slip away to an area of your home that relaxes you.

However, if you find that you're just not feeling up to the task no matter how much you try to get into the right frame of mind, *don't* perform the ritual. Sometimes saying no is a magical act. As a practitioner who has chosen to harness the forces that dwell

The Evil Eye

both within you and on the spiritual plane, you are responsible for a lot. Your magic will affect your own life as well as the lives of other people, and it's imperative that you maintain a healthy balance between your own needs and the needs of those you are seeking to help.

The third point is all about education—*your* education as a practitioner. It will undoubtedly improve with practice, but don't feel discouraged if your first few attempts to remove the Evil Eye produce less-than-stellar results. You're going to come across a situation where a friend or loved one says, "I feel really strange. Bad headache. And I'm tired. And you wouldn't believe the bad luck I've been having!" You will, of course, recognize all of the above as signs that the Eye has struck, and you will immediately reach for your go-to ritual in hopes of diagnosing it. Then you'll go about removing it, following the right steps and perhaps even sensing a real energy shift in the room. But an hour later, your friend or loved one will report that their symptoms have worsened as they head off to the medicine cabinet with a frown.

Disappointing, yes, but there's a lesson to be learned here. Some cases of the Evil Eye are worse than others and might require a stronger response. You may have to do the removal ritual two or three more times before anything changes, or you may have to choose one of the more elaborate spells to perform. Always remember that it's perfectly fine if you don't feel comfortable undertaking a more extensive magical approach.

In a scenario where you don't think you'll able to help someone who is clearly a victim of the Eye, offer to bless an amulet or talisman and give the amulet to them. And then keep up with your own practice. Don't let discouragement cloud what you already know to be true about your power: if you took on the work of learning how to remove the Evil Eye, it's because you have been called to do so, and every calling is rooted in divinity.

BEFORE YOU BEGIN

There are many ways to remove and banish the Evil Eye, and what follows are spells, rituals, prayers, and incantations solely for that purpose. What makes magic so spectacular is that it can be found in nearly every religious and spiritual tradition. You will also find practices that have no religious or spiritual affiliation, as well as spells and rituals for individual situations.

Peruse the following pages with an open mind and heart. You may be interested in Jewish spells, for example, but a Hindu one may also resonate with you. Follow your intuition and embrace whatever magic calls to you.

PROTECTING YOURSELF

Self-protection is one of the cornerstones of any magical practice. The following protection potion was handed down to me several years after I had learned to remove the Evil Eye; it's a simple mixture, but it works to help form a shield around you, minimizing the potential to absorb any negative residue. I anoint myself with it before I begin any ritual.

Warning: If you are pregnant, nursing, or seeking to conceive, don't use this particular infusion. Rue can cause uterine contractions, and rosemary is believed to be an "abortive" herb in two of the folk magic traditions I was trained in. Instead of using the ingredients below, use your own holy water, which does not contain any herbs that may be unsafe in these circumstances.

You will need:

- A pot

- A Mason jar

- Two cups of water

- A teaspoon of hyssop

- A teaspoon of rue

- Three sprigs of rosemary

- Three bay leaves

- Three pinches of salt

- A teaspoon of *Liquore Strega* or vodka

Add the water to the pot and boil. Wait at least ten minutes for the water to cool down a bit, then add the herbs. Allow the mixture to steep for two hours. Strain the infused water into the jar. Add the Liquore Strega (or vodka) and salt. Take several deep breaths. When you feel sufficiently calm and centered, place both of your hands around the jar and recite the following incantation:

Spirit to blood, Stone to Sky, the angel's sword is raised on high.
Circle and shield, from day to night, I stand protected in God's sight.

With your dominant hand, knock three times on the side of the jar. Then dip your index and middle fingers into it and anoint yourself. The anointing can be any gesture with which you feel comfortable. I make the sign of the cross, for example, but it's just as effective if you touch your forehead, the base of your throat and the center of your chest in a straight line. A friend of mine who uses this infusion anoints only her forehead and eyelids. I also know a witch who draws a pentagram over herself: left nipple to forehead, forehead to right nipple, right nipple to left shoulder, left shoulder to right shoulder, right shoulder back to the left nipple.

Pay close attention to the incantation. The first line refers to the link we have with our own ancestral heritage. I was taught to honor those who came before us, and in reciting those three simple words—*spirit to blood*—you are summoning the strength of your ancestors and awakening the power of their essence, which truly does course through your body. The second line invokes the natural forces of Earth, from the stones in the soil to the air, moisture, and light of the sky. The Archangel Michael isn't mentioned directly, but he's associated with protection and is commonly depicted with a sword. A circle signifies completion; like a womb, it shields what it holds while creating balance and sustenance. In the final lines of the incantation, you are projecting a clear image of yourself as one who is "watched over" by God. The reference to sight is about the eyes, and when you stand in direct view of the divine, your own eyes are able to see what isn't there to be seen.

Once you've anointed yourself, seal the jar and place it out of sight—in a kitchen cabinet, perhaps, or on a counter where it will not be immediately visible to anyone but you. The jar can also be placed on your altar if you have one. It's a simple ritual, and it adds a needed layer of spiritual protection to your magical work. In fact, I anoint myself with this infusion before meetings or social gatherings, especially if I'm going to be interacting with new people. You can also anoint the front and back doors of your home and your windows with it.

THE MAGIC

The following spells and rituals are to be done only after you have determined that you (or a friend, loved one, colleague) have been afflicted with the Evil Eye. In the previous chapter, you learned several ways to diagnose it and are hopefully comfortable with your chosen method. If the Evil Eye is at work, the proof will show up.

However, your whereabouts will determine the kind of magic you'll be performing. If you're sitting on the couch when your best friend texts to tell you about how weird she's feeling, you have quite a few options at hand in terms of diagnosing *and* curing the Evil Eye. You're at home and don't have to worry about averting the curious stares of strangers. It's also likely that you have in a cabinet or drawer the accoutrements needed to carry out a more elaborate spell or ritual. Where magic is concerned, being in a place where you feel comfortable and "at home" always helps.

SPIRITS AND SAINTS

One of the most significant lessons you will learn as a magical practitioner is that you have many allies. I'm not referring to your fellow witches, shamans, priests, or priestesses. I'm referring to the angels, saints, spirits, ancestors, and deities who inhabit the other realm. Though not always visible to the naked eye, they are present and, for the most part, happy to offer us assistance when we need it. We become more aware of our otherworldly allies when we make the conscious decision to do so.

What does that mean? It means making the time to light a candle and pray for five or ten minutes. It means putting away your phone to sit in silence for a certain amount of time. Yes, every single day. Once you are comfortable with your own self, you come to the realization that you are never really alone. And when the gravity of that realization truly hits home, you will begin to sense your spirit allies easily. What will you ask of them? How will you honor them in return? It's a reciprocal relationship. It will also be among the truest and most rewarding relationships you will ever experience in this lifetime.

When people hear the word *saint*, they tend to automatically think of Catholic iconography. In fact, saints belong to other

Christian denominations (like Eastern Orthodox) and also come from other religions. What makes someone a saint? In most cases, a saint is a person who was extraordinarily close to God and exemplified great virtue, kindness, courage, and strength. As you'll see from the following selection, not all saints spent their lives in monasteries tending to the poor or bending their knees in prayer. To be a saint is to be powerful—not only for God, but for your fellow human being.

In magical practice, the saints possess a particularly unique role. They are powerful intercessors who act as gateways to God, carrying our prayers and pleas for divine intervention straight to the source. Most Catholics will readily admit to having an affinity with, or a sense of "closeness" to, at least one saint, although it is not unusual for several saints to be revered. Many magical practitioners who have no connection to Catholicism also work with the saints. The men and women who appear in the paintings of Michelangelo, da Vinci, and Caravaggio—and on laminated holy cards—inspire a kind of devotion that can best be described as intensely personal. People feel comforted by the saints, which makes perfect sense. The saints were human; they were extraordinary individuals, but they lived and experienced the same struggles, joys, and—yes—superstitions as we do.

Spirits have a broader definition. Some have had an earthly existence and some have not. The archangels, goddesses Hekate and Aphrodite, gods Dionysus and Pan, and the djinn are all examples of spirits that have never had a corporeal presence. The ancestors are both the ancient ones who helped shape humanity as a whole and our recently departed loved ones; once of flesh and bone, they are now ethereal beings. While saints are generally attached (or assigned) to a specific cause, spirits have a broader remit. If you are looking for an amulet that you misplaced, it would be wise to petition Saint Anthony of Padua, the patron of lost items (among other things). If you want a secret to be revealed, or a certain truth to be brought to light, you might pray to the goddess Athena, who is linked to sight, eyes, and that which is hidden from view.

When combating the Evil Eye, saints and spirits are particularly effective; they exist at the crossroads where our world and the spiritual realm intersect, which grants them the unique ability to be fully present when we petition them. Saint and spirit magic illustrates a vital point: the magical and the mundane exist alongside each other, parallel but conjoined; they are not "worlds" apart.

You will feel the assistance of whichever saint or spirit you call upon. Sometimes they make themselves known through a strong and very pleasant scent, a gust of wind, or a quick knock on the wall. I've known practitioners who were moved to tears and wept joyfully for several minutes after calling on a saint or spirit. A fellow practitioner from Spain has told me that he experiences auditory phenomena shortly after performing any kind of saint magic; he always hears his name being called when he walks outside the next day, or he hears someone speak the name of the saint he petitioned. It's thrilling to receive this kind of confirmation, but it doesn't happen in every instance. Making a connection with a saint or spirit is something that occurs interiorly, and the more you work with them, the stronger that connection will become.

Amadou Bamba

Born in Senegal in 1853, Amadou Bamba was a scholar, mystic, and religious leader who played a vital role in converting scores of people to Islam. He founded the Mouride Brotherhood (also known as the Mouride Way), which is based on his own sacred teachings. Still practiced today, Mouridism encourages peaceful living through charity, humility, and the principal of working to support one's family. Amadou was persecuted by the French and exiled to Gabon in 1895 and then Mauritania in 1902. Despite these hardships, he never thought himself a prisoner. Instead, he believed his mission in life was divinely inspired.

Aboard a ship during captivity, he was told that he didn't have permission to pray. In response, Amadou flung his prayer rug overboard and then climbed down into the waters after it. Onlookers took this as suicide, but the Archangel Gabriel soon appeared and, with the help of other angels, held up the prayer rug on which Amadou prayed. Later he was exiled to a tiny island in the sea swarming with unfriendly *djinn;* he calmed them and managed to flee. Only one image of Amadou exists; it is believed to bestow blessings and grant protection. It is also known to expel the Evil Eye. To petition him, meditate on his image while reciting one of his poems.

Athena

An ancient Greek goddess, Athena is most frequently associated with wisdom, but she is also a deity of strength, courage, battle, and war. She is depicted as a beautiful woman holding a spear and a shield. Though she also wears a cape adorned with serpents, she is more commonly linked with the owl, a bird known for its extraordinary ability to see in darkness. According to legend, Athena appeared on battlefields as an owl. Can her origins be traced back to Libyan traditions of the Great Mother? Many scholars support this theory. She presides over women's mysteries and fertility but also over the realms of death and rebirth. She may also have been a primordial eye goddess, staring out at humanity with unerring vision. The snake, the spider, the wolf, and the horse have also been linked to her.

Though Athena can be petitioned for just about anything, it is especially wise for brides and grooms to invoke her protection against the Evil Eye on their wedding day. It is believed that Athena will "keep watch" over a wedding ceremony, smiting envious glances and ensuring that the couple has a smooth path to conception. To petition Athena, light two yellow candles and make an offering that includes one or more of the following: wine, honey, pomegranates, olives, crescent-shaped cookies, and pears. Invoke her using images of owls, serpents, or spiders. For her protection against the Evil Eye at all times, fill a pouch will pomegranate seeds and strands of your own hair and carry it as an amulet.

Ayizan

A supremely ancient and powerful *lwa* —the sacred spirits of Vodou—Ayizan presides over the marketplace and other public spaces. She may be represented by mounds of dirt and palm leaves, symbolizing the sacredness of the earth. Believed to be the spirit of the first mambo (Vodou priestess), Ayizan protects against the Evil Eye, assists in cleansing spaces of negative or stagnant energy, and exorcises malevolent spirits from her devotees. Ayizan is incredibly powerful and commands the utmost respect. She punishes those who exploit the young, the vulnerable, and the poor. Ayizan is a matron of women. Her knowledge of the spirit world is vast and deep, but she should always be honored first when it comes to rituals. To petition her, make offerings of spring water, palm leaves, plantains, and white flowers. Light a silver candle and pray to Ayizan in the doorways of your home, asking her to deflect the Evil Eye.

Baubo

To the ancient Greeks and Romans, the act of exposing one's private parts was considered a defensive gesture, especially against the Evil Eye. One theory is that this scared away the demon that fueled the Eye's strength. If ever there was an image that solidified the significance of exposing one's genitals, it is that of the goddess

Baubo. Greek in origin, Baubo is the matron of female humor and the belly laugh—both of which represent an important phase of healing. In fact, in Greek mythology it is Baubo who exposes her vulva to the goddess Demeter, which causes Demeter to laugh and begin to let go of her grief. As such, Baubo is a trickster with a very tender and compassionate side. She is not a maiden but a crone, despite her associations with fertility.

Baubo connects only with women and female energy; as such, she is considered one of the *Bona Dea*. Images of Baubo depict her in the act of exposing her vulva or as a figure comprised of long legs and a head—a kind of walking vagina, with nipples for eyes and a vulva for a mouth. These depictions were meant to accentuate the power of female sexuality and laughter as a healing modality; with the advent of Christianity, however, images of Baubo were branded pornographic and thus expunged from most sources of mythology.

Baubo is a protector of women, babies, and children. Wearing an amulet that bears her image immediately deflects the Evil Eye. Interestingly, the act for which she is known—raising her dress to expose her vulva—is referred to as *ana-suromai*, which in itself is an image that appears on amulets.

Bes

A deity of music, dancing, love, and general domestic bliss, Bes was widely worshipped in ancient Egypt. He is also a great protector of pregnant women, children, and childbirth. Images of him depict a small man with an unruly beard and a lion's mane, often holding or playing drums. He is sometimes described as grotesque on account of his demonic grin and pointy ears. In general, Bes has a wild, fun demeanor; he's loud—so loud that his antics are believed to ward away demons and negative energy. He also carries a knife and a *Sa*—a protective symbol in ancient Egypt.

Hanging an image of Bes in the bedroom of a home will keep a relationship active and joyful. In a child's bedroom, his iconography ensures safety. Pregnant women who wear an amulet of Bes are protected from the Evil Eye and envious or resentful glances. Female entertainers—especially dancers and musicians—are also under the guardianship of Bes.

Ganesha

In the pantheon of Hindu deities, one of the most revered and worshipped is Ganesha. Easily identified by his elephant head, his image can be found across India and in other parts of the world as well, and his worship extends to Jains and Buddhists. Ganesha is primarily known as the remover of obstacles and bringer of good luck. He is associated with new beginnings and is the deva (divine being) of wisdom and intelligence. According to Hindu mythology, he is the son of Parvati and Shiva, but because of his popularity among devotees, he is considered a pan-Hindu god.

Wearing an amulet of Ganesha is considered highly auspicious by Hindus. He will eliminate obstacles and remove difficulties from one's path, and this includes negative energy in the form of the Evil Eye. Some believe his trunk distracts the Eye; others believe his trunk acts in a defensive gesture to cast it away. Ganesha is associated with the Hindu mantra Om/Aum, and according to Kundalini yoga he resides in the root chakra. It is best to put on a Ganesha amulet at the start of the day, whatever time that might be; as the god of new beginnings, Ganesha will ensure protection as he clears the paths ahead of you.

Prayer to Saint Benedict

Like many saints, Saint Benedict waged a battle against demons and was intimately acquainted with the debilitating power of evil.

Thus, he is known as the patron of exorcisms and is petitioned for all matters relating to protection from supernatural forces. Reciting the following prayer aloud will banish the Eye's energy.

My Dear St. Benedict, I call upon your power and compassion in this moment of need. Please hear me. At this time, I require protection from evil, negativity, and the vindictive thoughts of those who wish me harm. With the cross of Jesus Christ as my guide, I implore you to intercede for me. Please ask God to protect me and to protect my home, property, and possessions today and always. Bestow upon me your holy blessing and make certain that I am kept safely in the hands of our Lord and under the mantle of the Blessed Virgin Mary. Deliver me from danger, oppression, prejudice, illness and accidents, envy and greed, hatred and ill will. Deliver me from malevolent forces seen and unseen. I ask this in the name of Jesus Christ. Amen.

Prayer to San Luis Beltran to Remove the Evil Eye

Born in Valenica, Spain, in 1526, Luis Beltran was a Dominican friar known for his zeal and his dedication to preaching the gospel. He served the sick and dying during the plague of 1557. Shortly thereafter, he set sail for South America, where he developed a large ministry that converted thousands to Catholicism and even drew the attention of Saint Teresa of Avila. Legend has it that San Luis walked on the waters of Cienga da Manzanillo and had the ability to end droughts. His cult is especially strong in Cuba, where he is known as the (unofficial) patron saint of the Evil Eye.

Anyone afflicted by the Eye should recite this prayer three times:

My dear San Luis, ever mindful of the Lord's majesty and strength, I implore your intercession here and now. I call upon our Blessed

Mother Mary, ever compassionate, to assist you. I call upon the angels and archangels of the celestial court to assist you. Right now, in this sacred moment, heal this afflicted child of God [recite the name of the afflicted individual] of this disease; of the Evil Eye; of all pain, accidents, and dangers plaguing them; and of the spears of another's envy. San Luis, my beloved brother: heal [name of the afflicted] in the name of our Lord and savior, Jesus Christ. Amen.

Precious Blood Blessing

This simple ritual to remove the Evil Eye utilizes nothing more than the power of blessing and anointing. It is to be performed when the afflicted individual is with you. If you are the one suffering from the Eye's effects, you can do this ritual for yourself. If you can't reach around to the back of your neck, simply anoint the front of your body.

You will need:

• A shot glass

• One tablespoon of red wine

• A pinch of salt

Begin by making the sign of the cross. Pour the wine into the shot glass, add the salt to the wine, then bless it by reciting the Litany of the Precious Blood of Jesus, which is readily available to read online.

If you are removing the Eye from someone else, face them and ask them to close their eyes. Dip your right thumb into the wine and anoint them by making the sign of the cross over their forehead, the center of their chest, and the back of their neck.

Instruct the individual to open their eyes. Hand them the shot glass and have them dip the tip of their own right thumb into the wine. Then they should anoint themselves by making a cross over each of their eyelids.

Saint Elijah

The Jewish prophet Elijah is venerated as a saint by both the Eastern Orthodox and Roman Catholic churches. Elijah is frequently depicted as an older bearded man being carried up to Heaven in a flaming chariot, which is drawn by flaming horses. The image is based on the biblical account of Elijah's ascent to Heaven; however, it also closely resembles ancient Greek images of their solar deity, Helios. Some scholars and theologians believe that images of the Christian saint were syncretized from a pagan sky deity or Perun, the Russian thunder god of sky, lightning, storms, and rain. These latter attributes remained with Saint Elijah, as he possesses the power to end droughts.

Saint Elijah the Prophet Water is a powerful potion made from rain collected on either July 20th or 30th. The sacred water is known to protect against the Evil Eye. Mark those two dates on your calendar, and when they come around, invoke Saint Elijah. He may respond and send you a rainstorm. If so, collect the rain any way you can and preserve it. Label and refrigerate it. Use it sparingly but whenever you feel the effects of the Eye on yourself, your home, or your loved ones. Thankfully, only a few drops are needed to repel negativity.

Saint Lucy

Saint Lucy's story is a gory one. She was a Christian martyr executed during the Diocletianic Persecution, the last and largest effort in the Roman Empire to expunge Christianity. She was born to a noble family in the city of Syracuse, on the island of Sicily, circa 280 CE and consecrated her virginity to God at a very early age. While it's difficult to separate fact from legend, the most commonly held belief is that Saint Lucy (Lucia) gouged her own eyes to discourage a suitor's romantic interest in her. Another theory states that the Governor of Syracuse ultimately ordered her eyes to be gouged as punishment for speaking out against him. As her body was being prepared for burial, it was discovered that her eyes had been miraculously restored. Lucy is the patron saint of the blind, as well as those who suffer from eye ailments.

In art, Saint Lucy is frequently depicted holding a golden tray upon which two eyeballs rest—the eyes she allegedly gouged from her own sockets. In this popular image, however, her face is beautiful and whole, unmarred by violence. The image tells the story of a miracle. Because Saint Lucy is associated with eyes, she is an excellent saint to call upon when working to remove the Evil Eye. The following ritual can be used whenever you want to remove it.

You will need:

- A plate

- Two cloves of garlic (peeled)

- Two pins

- Two handfuls of salt

Place the plate on a hard surface. Take the cloves of garlic and set them side by side on the plate. When you look at them, you'll notice that they resemble the shape of human eyes. Take several deep breaths and center yourself. Look down at the plate and make the sign of the cross. Then place your hands over the cloves and recite the following incantation:

> Saint Lucy my light, Saint Lucy my guide, come to my assistance and stand at my side.

Pick up one of the pins with your dominant hand, securely pinching the blunt end, and blow on it. Using your other hand, hold the clove on the right side of the plate with your thumb and forefinger. Slowly and carefully insert the pin into the clove and say:

For the envy sent and the malice intended, for the wounds and thoughts now perfectly mended, eye to the needle, burst and bust, needle to the eye, dust to dust.

When the clove is sufficiently pierced, let it rest on the plate with the pin still in it. Pick up the second pin, blow on it, and then hold the second clove just as you did the first. As you insert the needle into the second clove, say:

Light of Saint Lucy, heal what's maligned, balance restored as evil eyes go blind. Light of Saint Lucy, bright as the sun, look down from heaven and let it be done.

Put the second pierced clove on the plate beside the first. With the handfuls of salt, use your dominant hand to make a cross over the plate, seeing to it that the salt touches the cloves. Look away from the plate and make the sign of the cross. The ritual is done.

Leave the plate out for an hour. When you're ready, carefully extract the needles from the cloves, wipe them clean, and put them in a safe place, as they can be reused. (I deposit mine in a salt-filled bowl that sits on my altar.) Wrap the cloves of garlic in foil, folding the sheet away from you. Dispose of the packet immediately—preferably somewhere outside. You can also smash the cloves before wrapping them.

Of note: If you start crying after finishing the ritual, don't hold back the emotion; let it run its course. It's a sure sign from Saint Lucy that your work was successful. Touch the tears that flow from your eyes and anoint yourself with them. The tears you shed are a blessing.

Ojos de Santa Lucia

Despite its garish ending, the story of Saint Lucy is ultimately about courage and the power of faith. Yes, Lucy's eyes (allegedly) ended up on a plate, but for millions of people around the world, those eyes have become symbols of divine protection. The *ojos* (also referred to as *ojitos*) are small eye-shaped beads fastened to a pin to form a brooch; sometimes a piece of red coral is affixed to the brooch, and sometimes the eye beads are black and red, not the traditional blue-and-white color of the nazar. In Cuba and South America, affixing the amulet to an infant or child is a popular practice because infants and children are particularly susceptible to the Evil Eye. The *ojo* amulet is also worn as a bracelet. It is not uncommon for adults to carry them in their pocket and purses or on key chains.

The ojos smite envious glances and baneful energy and are believed by some to enhance intuition, especially if danger is lurking nearby. Primarily a Catholic amulet, the Ojos de Santa Lucia are also popular among practitioners of Regla Lucumi (Santeria).

Saint Odile

The daughter of the duke of Alsace and his wife, Odile was born blind and immediately rejected by her father. When he plotted to kill his infant daughter, her mother came to the rescue, either entrusting Odile to a local peasant family or placing her in a basket and floating her down the river. Legend has it that when she was twelve, Odile received a visit from Saint Erhard, who had been guided to her by an angel. A miracle worker, Saint Erhard restored Odile's vision. Odile's initial attempts to reconcile with her father were unsuccessful. Her brother tried to advance the process (mainly for his own selfish reasons), but the young man's mission ended in tragedy: he was soon killed by his and Odile's own father. Odile resurrected her brother and then fled. Later, she and her father reconciled, and the duke built a convent for Odile atop what is today called Mont Sainte-Odile in France. A second convent was built near a miraculous spring; Odile was directed to this holy site by Saint John the Baptist.

Like Saint Lucy, Odile is depicted holding her own eyes—not on a plate, but on a book. She is also a patron of eyes and eye illnesses. Because her sight was miraculously restored, her association with vision is especially powerful. She is even invoked by psychics, clairvoyants, and fortunetellers. Anyone suffering from the effects of the Evil Eye can petition Saint Odile to banish negative energy. Simply dedicate a white chime candle to her, inscribe your name (or the name of the afflicted individual) into the wax, and light it. Let it burn down completely.

Saint Therese of Lisieux Crossed Roses Spell

She has been called the most popular saint of modern times, and for good reason. Saint Therese of the Child Jesus and the Holy Face—commonly known as Saint Therese of Lisiuex—was a Carmelite nun in France who lived a cloistered life. In her autobiography, *The Story of a Soul*, she wrote about her own particular devotion to God, which came to be known as "the little way" because of its purity and simple surrender to the love of Jesus Christ. Therese died of tuberculosis in 1897, at the age of twenty-four. Her autobiography, published posthumously, quickly became a towering volume of Catholic spirituality. She was canonized in 1925 and named a Doctor of the Church in 1997. On her deathbed, it was reported that Therese said: "I will spend my heaven doing good on earth. I will let fall from heaven a shower of roses."

She has remained true to that promise. Millions of people around the world are fiercely devoted to Saint Therese and thousands of miracles have been attributed to her intercession. The French singer Edith Piaf claimed to have been cured of blindness following a visit to Therese's tomb. In the book *Stronger Than Steel: Soldiers of the Great War Write to Saint Therese of Lisieux*, the letters of numerous soldiers (mainly French) who battled the horrors of the Great War give testimony to the saint's incredible power; many of these letters detail apparitions of St. Therese on the battlefield. The book's title is apt. Therese is known as the Little Flower because of the compassion and softness of her writings, but anyone who has prayed to her knows that she is, indeed, a force to be reckoned with.

The following spell to remove the Evil Eye reflects the "gentle steeliness" of Saint Therese. Though she undoubtedly touched the divine in her lifetime, she was admittedly prone to the foibles and pitfalls that all people experience. Therese was deeply human and understood the pain of loss, as well as the disturbing nature of jealousy and cruelty. This spell is especially effective when removing the Evil Eye from a child, but I have used it countless times for myself and other adults.

You will need:

- A holy card or picture of Saint Therese (a digital picture is fine if you don't have access to a holy card or printer)

- Two red roses

- A small nail (preferably iron, but the standard steel sold in hardware stores is fine too)

- One pink or red candle (votive or chime)

- A candleholder or plate

- Matches or a lighter

- Red ribbon or twine

Gather all the items and make sure they are at arm's reach before beginning the spell. Be certain to trim the roses of any thorns. When you are ready, take the holy card or image of Saint Therese and set it down on a flat surface. Make the sign of the cross and spend at least a minute concentrating on the image. Connect with it. If you've never worked with Saint Therese, begin by simply telling her why it is you are calling on her for assistance.

Pick up the candle. While holding it, recite one Glory Be. Place the candle in a holder or, if it's a votive, on a plate. Light it.

Pick up the roses, holding one in each hand. Looking again at the image of St. Therese, say:

Walk me to the garden, take me to the altar, in your presence none can falter. Beloved Therese, the Little Flower, imbue this spell with your power.

Place the roses down on the surface, crossing the stems so that they form an X. Say aloud the name of the afflicted person.

Carefully pluck one petal off of each rose, and then make a kind of packet by tying the nail in the rose petals with the ribbon or string. It doesn't have to be neat and tidy; what's important is that the nail is tucked in between the rose petals. Set this charm down over the image of Saint Therese (or in front of it, if you're using a digital image) and then make the sign of the cross to close the spell.

Leave the charm there until the candle burns down completely; afterwards, move the charm to a safe place, where it must remain for twenty-four hours. Place the roses in a vase and tend to them.

When twenty-four hours have passed, unwrap the nail from within the ribbon and rose petals and use the nail to hang up a picture in your home. (If you've performed this spell for someone else, give that person the nail with the same instructions.) The picture should be of your choosing, but it's generally a good idea to select one of yourself or loved ones. Save the ribbon or twine—you can reuse it the next time you perform the spell.

Of note: Saint Therese is in constant communication with those who pray to her, and she will absolutely let you know that she heard you. After performing this spell, keep your eyes open because you'll see a rose somewhere. It might appear on a napkin, on someone's T-shirt, or on the bumper sticker of the car in front of you. You might also walk into a restaurant and find out that your waitress's name is Theresa or Rose. It's a sign that Saint Therese is with you—and that your prayer has been answered.

Spell Against All Evils

The following spell doesn't require many tools or ingredients, and it includes one of the lesser known—but immensely powerful—Catholic prayers. According to some theologians, the Prayer Against All Evils is usually recited at exorcisms. You certainly don't need to be battling a demon to use it, but read it over several times before putting it to use so that you become familiar with the wording. This prayer is believed to be impervious to all negative influences; it invokes more than the saints, but I have included it here because of its intercessory nature. When said with a calm mind and a faithful heart, it vanquishes the effects of the Evil Eye and immediately restores balance to the afflicted.

You will need:

• A cup or bowl filled with water

• Three kitchen matches and accompanying strike-on-box

At your altar, kitchen counter, or preferred table, set the cup of water and the box of matches before you. Remove three matches and line them up neatly. Take several deep breaths. Make the sign of the cross and recite the following:

Spirit of our God, Father, Son, and Holy Spirit, Most Holy Trinity, Immaculate Virgin Mary, angels, archangels, and saints of heaven, descend upon me. Please purify me, Lord. Banish all the forces of evil from me, destroy them, defeat them, so that I can be healthy and do good deeds. Banish from me all spells, witchcraft, black magic, maledictions, and the evil eye; diabolic infestations, oppressions, possessions; all that is evil and sinful, jealousy, perfidy, envy; physical, psychological, moral, spiritual, diabolical aliments. Burn all these evils in hell, that they may never again touch me or any other creature in the entire world. I command and bid all the powers who molest me—by the power of God all powerful, in the name of Jesus Christ our Savior, through the intercession of the Immaculate Virgin Mary—to leave me forever, and to be consigned into the everlasting hell, where they will be bound by Saint Michael the archangel, Saint Gabriel, Saint Raphael, our guardian angels, and where they will be crushed under the heel of the Immaculate Virgin Mary. Amen.

Take the first match and strike it against the box. As the flame burns, recite the Lord's Prayer. You should be finished before the flame reaches your fingertips, and at the end of the prayer, plunge the match into the bowl or cup of water.

With the second lit match, recite a Hail Mary and repeat the above process.

With the third lit match, recite a Glory Be and repeat the same above process.

Close the ritual by making the sign of the cross. Dispose of the water and the burnt matches outside of your home. Once you've either dumped everything in a trash bin or buried the items, turn around, stomp your feet on the ground three times, and then walk away without looking back.

To Remove the Evil Eye from Your Home

Stand in the doorway of every room and recite Psalm 121:1–8. You can find many of the psalms and prayers referenced in this book in the online resources section of the bibliography.

JEWISH MAGIC

The Evil Eye is prominent in Jewish tradition. Called the *ayin hara* in Hebrew and the *ayin hora* in Yiddish, it appears in rabbinic literature of the first few centuries CE and plays a significant, if slightly veiled, role in Jewish culture today. It is common for Jewish people to say certain phrases or spit three times—*tfu, tfu, tfu*—after mentioning specific plans or discussing positive developments that have occurred in one's life. If you've ever seen the classic film *Fiddler on the Roof*, you'll see this practice in action by the mother of the family, Golde.

The Talmud or oral law, the compendium of Jewish law and legends, offers a ritual to confront the powers of the Evil Eye: "One who enters a city and fears the evil eye should hold the thumb of his right hand in his left hand and the thumb of his left hand in his right hand and recite the following: I, so-and-so son of so-and-so, come from the descendants of Joseph, over whom the evil eye has no dominion." (Berakhot 55b)

In *The Encyclopedia of Jewish Myth, Magic, and Mysticism*, Rabbi Geoffrey Dennis writes:

> Judaism is one of the oldest living esoteric traditions in the world. Virtually every form of Western mysticism and spiritualism known today draws upon Jewish mythic and occult teachings—magic, prayer, angelology, alchemy, numerology, astral projection, dream interpretation, astrology, amulets, divination, altered states of consciousness, alternative healing and rituals of power— all have roots in the Jewish occult.

Ben Porat Yosef Spell

A very powerful amulet in Judaism is the Ben Porat Yosef. According to the Torah, when the patriarch Jacob was dying, he blessed each of his sons. The blessing he gave to Joseph was reduced over time to the phrase *ben porat yosef* (translated from Hebrew it means *a fruitful son*), which comprises the first three words of the blessing. The blessing has evolved into a saying to ward off the Evil Eye, envy, and jealousy that is especially popular among Sephardic Jews, the Jews of the Spanish diaspora.

You will need:

- One white candle

- One candleholder

- Matches or a lighter

- A Ben Porat Yosef amulet (a photo of one can be substituted) or laminated card

Begin by taking several deep breaths. When you are ready, light the candle. Wait another minute or so, allowing yourself to focus on God's presence. Then recite this line from the opening of the *Amidah*, the central prayer in Jewish liturgy:

Adonai, open my lips so I may speak Your praise.

Pick up the Ben Porat Yosef. Visually trace the writing and the sacred symbols. Now recite Genesis 49:22:

Joseph is a fruitful bough, Even a fruitful bough by a well; Whose branches run over the wall.

If you are performing the spell for yourself, press the charm (or copy of the charm) against your forehead three times. Set it down and pick up the candle. Carefully make three circles around your head with the candle. Go slowly so that the wax doesn't drip and burn your skin. Set the candle down and pick up the Ben Porat Yosef, and again press it to your forehead. Now recite the following:

Remove the evil that surrounds me. Hold me in the shadow of your wings, O God, who watches over me and delivers me. May the

words of my mouth and meditations of my heart be pleasing to You,
Adonai, my Rock and my Redeemer.

Place the Ben Porat Yosef down and extinguish the candle. The spell is done.

If you are performing the spell for someone else, simply repeat the exact steps on the person. The amulet can now be worn or carried.

Cloves of Protection Spell

Aromatic and pungent, cloves are a popular spice in many types of cuisine. A lesser known fact is that cloves possess extraordinary magical properties, especially when it comes to protection and cleansing. Look closely at a clove and you will see that it resembles a nail, able to pierce the Evil Eye. When combined with water, cloves also absorb negativity. Use the following spell to banish the Evil Eye quickly.

You will need:

• A glass of water

• Eighteen whole cloves

• One white candle

• Candleholder

• A lighter or matches

Begin by lighting the candle. Stand for a few minutes in the flame's glow and ask for God's blessing. Hold the glass (filled with water) level with the flame and recite Numbers 6:24–26.

Set the glass down. Take the cloves and drop them, one by one, into the glass. In Judaism, every word has a numerical value, and eighteen is the number of life—*chai*—and the cloves will simultaneously burn away the Evil Eye and restore balance to your mind and body. Leave the glass next to the candle for eighteen minutes (set a timer!) and then extinguish the candle.

Dispose of the entire contents of the glass—water and cloves—outside of your home.

The Hashkiveinu

The second blessing following the Shema during Maariv (evening prayers), the Hashkiveinu is a prayer that asks God to grant us a restful night; it asks for shelter and peace and defense against our enemies. Many of the Jewish individuals I interviewed told me that they prayed the Hashkiveinu whenever they felt anxious or angry—and especially when they knew the *ayin hara* was at work in their lives.

Rachel, a doctor in Los Angeles, uses the prayer to "reset her life" whenever she feels consumed by negativity. "There's a big difference—to me, at least—between the exhaustion that follows a long day and the exhaustion that follows a long *bad* day," she explained. "Prayer is restorative, and sometimes feeling that cloak of protection is the best medicine."

When Aaron, a graduate student in New York City, was in college, he started praying the Hashkiveinu following a particularly difficult time in his life. Two years earlier, his grandmother's neighbor had diagnosed him with *ayin hora*; she performed a ritual to remove it and then suggested that he begin praying regularly. "There are lots of beautiful prayers in Judaism," he said. "But the Hashkiveinu is especially beautiful because it asks God to give us what we truly need—rest. We get that rest because we know that we're protected and safe from harm as we shut down for the day and enter the night. When you pray the Hashkiveinu before going to sleep, every breath you take is blessed, and your body is being cleansed of the negativity that would otherwise impede a restful slumber."

There are no specific instructions to pray the Hashkiveinu. You can light a candle and stand in front of it, or you can simply read the prayer while lying in bed. The Hashkiveinu can be found in Hebrew, English, and other translations in many Jewish prayer books and online.

Morning Prayer

If you feel the Evil Eye has invaded your life, one of the simplest and strongest ways to dispel it is through the recitation of morning prayers. Prayers can center your thoughts, cleanse your energy, and set the tone for the day. Make every effort to spend a few minutes alone every morning with prayers from the *Birkhot Ha-Shahar* (early morning blessings), which can be found in Jewish prayer books and online.

Psalm Spells

The Book of Psalms—known as *Tehillim* in the Hebrew Scriptures—is often used by Jewish people as part of their personal prayers and supplications. When illness strikes, when relationships fall apart, or when someone is going through a difficult time, the Psalms can be a spiritual balm, providing both comfort and courage. The Psalms have also long played a significant role in Jewish magic, especially where matters of health, healing, and protection are concerned. In Kabbalistic magical practice, Psalm 121 is often used as an amulet against demons.

The following spells should be performed after the Evil Eye has been diagnosed. Each spell makes use of a different Psalm, and you will be making your own personal amulet. You can find a copy of the mentioned Psalms online, in many Jewish prayer books, or in the *Tanakh* (a volume containing the Torah, Prophets, and Writings).

To remove the Evil Eye from your home

You will need:

- A white candle
- A candleholder
- Matches or a lighter
- A pinch of hyssop
- Piece of paper
- Pen
- Tape
- Psalm 91

Ideally, this spell should be performed at your kitchen table, but use the room or personal space in which you feel the calmest. When you are ready, arrange the items on the table in front of you.

Hold the candle between the palms of your hands and recite Psalm 91 out loud. Place the candle in its holder and light it. In the glow of the candlelight, reread the Psalm, this time silently to yourself. Copy the Psalm onto the blank sheet of paper, writing it out slowly with the pen. Take your time doing this—it might take as little as fifteen minutes or as long as two hours. Your writing doesn't have to be neat, nor does it matter if the ink smears a little. Concentrate only on the words of the Psalm. When you are done, take the hyssop and place it in the center of the paper. Carefully fold the paper in half, toward you and over the hyssop. Turn it right and fold it toward you again. Turn it right again and fold it toward you a third time. Seal the edges with the tape, making a kind of packet. Again, don't worry about keeping it neat. This is for your own personal use.

If you're using a chime candle, let it burn out completely. If you're using a taper candle, snuff it out. Holding the packet in your dominant hand, touch it to the front door of your home and at least one window in each room. You can place the packet in a kitchen drawer and leave it there for one month. Dispose of it by burning it in a fireplace or a fireproof bowl.

To remove the Evil Eye from yourself (personal healing)

You will need:

- A black candle

- A candleholder

- Matches or a lighter

- Paper

- A pen

- Tape

- Red string or cord, at least 12 inches in length

- Psalm 30

Hold the candle between the palms of your hands and recite Psalm 30 out loud. Place the candle in its holder and light it. In the glow of the candlelight, reread the Psalm, this time silently to yourself. Copy the Psalm onto the blank sheet of paper, writing it out slowly with the pen. Remember to take your time and go at your own pace.

When you have finished writing the psalm, focus on the piece of paper in front of you. Moisten the thumb of your right hand with your own saliva and then press your thumb to the top of the paper and then the bottom of the paper. Don't worry if the ink smears. Fold the paper toward you once. Using the pen, write your full name across the blank portion of the paper. Turn it to the right, fold it again, and again write your name on the blank portion of the paper. Turn it a third time to the right and write your name a third time. Use the tape to seal it, making a tight packet. Tie the red string or cord around the packet tightly. Don't worry about being neat.

Place the packet under your pillow and sleep on it for one night. You may also leave it on a bedside table. Carry the packet with you, preferably in a pocket so that it's close to your body, until the symptoms have subsided. To dispose of it, burn it in a fireplace or fireproof dish.

To remove the Evil Eye from a loved one

You will need:

- A blue candle

- A candleholder

- Matches or a lighter

- Paper

- A pen

- Tape

- A small pouch or charm bag

- A lock of the afflicted individual's hair

- A sprig of rue

- A sprig of rosemary

- Psalm 41

Hold the candle between the palms of your hands and recite Psalm 41 out loud. Place the candle in its holder and light it. In the glow of the candlelight, reread the Psalm, this time silently to yourself. Copy the Psalm onto the blank sheet of paper, writing it out slowly with the pen. Like with the previous spells, go at your own pace.

When you have finished writing the psalm, focus on the piece of paper in front of you. Fold the paper toward you once and turn it to the right. Fold it a second time and turn it to the right. Fold it a third time and turn it to the right again. Seal the packet with the tape, carefully going over the edges. Now fold the paper a fourth time and use pressure to flatten it against the table. Here, you can choose to roll the packet, albeit unevenly, until it resembles a scroll. Place it, along with the sprigs of rosemary and rue, into the pouch. Set the pouch in front of the candle until the candle burns out completely.

Give the pouch to the afflicted individual. If they live in your home, hang it in their bedroom. When the symptoms subside, take the sprigs of rue and rosemary from the pouch and burn them. Do not, however, burn the lock of hair; let it remain in the pouch, tightly sealed. Place the pouch somewhere safe and let it remain there.

PROTECTIONS IN ISLAM

As mentioned earlier, al-ayn—the Evil Eye—is prevalent among Muslims. While Islamic tradition holds that adherents should rely solely on God to keep them safe from sorcery, witchcraft, and evil spirits, the use of amulets and talismans is common among Muslims, as is reciting specific prayers or a ruqyah (incantation) from the Quran.

The Last Three Surahs of the Quran

To cure the Evil Eye, every night for seven nights recite the last four Surahs of the Quran: Surah Ikhlas, Surah Al-Kafirun, Surah Nas, and Surah Falaq.

Ruqyah Bath

As in most religious traditions, water is sacred and aids in healing of the body, mind, and spirit. A ruqyah bath is a common remedy for the Evil Eye, and it requires nothing more than a glass of water.

You may use the surahs listed in the above section or the following ruqyahs: Surah al-Fatihah, Ayatul al-Kursi, Surah Al A'raf. Recite the one of your choosing over a glass of water. While doing so, keep your mouth close to the water and then breathe or blow on it; ideally, particles of saliva should hit the water.

Now take a sip of the water.

Finally, add the remaining water to a bath. A ruqyah bath is most effective when done daily for three days, or until the symptoms of al-ayn subside.

Aside from the recitation of a *ruqya*, many Quranic verses are made into amulets and worn around the neck; they are sometimes also framed and hung in homes.

Nigerian Spell to Remove the Evil Eye

This simple ritual, given to me by a friend from Nigeria in her own native dialect of Igbo, uses nothing more than hand gestures and your own voice, so it's easily performed anywhere and at any time. Once you've detected the Evil Eye, perform the following steps.

Stop whatever you're doing and take three deep, strong breaths. Focus your eyes on something specific—a picture on the wall, a book on a shelf, a boat bobbing on the water in the distance. The point here is to really center yourself, and quickly.

Raise your right arm and make three circles above your head, snapping three times as you do so. Say aloud "Tufiakwa! Tufiakwa! Tufiakwa!" which means "God forbid!" When combined with the act of making circles above your head, it's believed that the Evil Eye gets caught up, confused, and weakened. When weak, the Eye can be flung away and its effects promptly thwarted.

GENERAL SPELLS

Back to You Spell

It happens all the time. You go to a special event—a dinner party, a wedding, or just about any social gathering—and you leave feeling "off" or just plain sick. Maybe you have a headache. Did you drop a plate when you got home? Something's not right, and when you think back to the event that you attended, you remember seeing or speaking to someone who wasn't particularly pleasant, or to people you know don't like you. If it's a family event, the chances are quite high that there's "bad blood" circulating. The Evil Eye has struck—and likely under the guise of a disingenuous smile or compliment. I have a friend who closes her eyes whenever a toast is announced and champagne glasses are raised because she believes it's the perfect moment for someone to "eye" you maliciously.

This simple spell is a personal favorite of mine. It's quick, easy, and as direct as you can get.

You will need:

• One wine glass

• One paper or plastic cup

- Bottle of wine (red or white)

You can perform the first part of this spell right at your kitchen counter or table. Set the wine glass and the paper or plastic cup on either side of the wine bottle. If you know who sent you the Evil Eye, concentrate on an image of the person you have in your mind's eye, or repeat their name silently to yourself three times. Pour some wine into the glass—you only need enough for about two sips or one decent gulp. Holding the glass in your dominant hand, recite the following incantation:

Mighty Dionysus of harvest and vine, I invoke your blessing as I drink this wine.

Raise the glass and "salute" the great god Dionysus. Take a long sip or a hearty gulp of the wine. Relish its flavor and feel its power as it warms your body. Set the glass aside.

Now pour wine into the paper or plastic cup. Holding the cup, go to your front door and open it. Look outside—at the sky or the grass or the ground. Don't look at a particular person, animal, or object; keep your gaze vague, but hold tight to the image of the person in your mind's eye. Raise the paper or plastic cup and say:

Mighty Dionysus of bull and horn, where there is a leaf now place a thorn. To my enemy, I raise a toast: drink back your malice, not the least but the most.

Spit into the cup three times. Carry the cup back into your house and dump the wine down a drain or into the toilet. Then throw the paper or plastic cup on the floor and stomp on it three times. Whether you're left with plastic shards or a severely deformed paper cup, carefully clean it all up and dispose outside.

The Fire Bath

Like all the elements, fire can be useful or destructive. In its capacity to cleanse and foster regeneration and growth, it is extremely potent. This simple spell derives from a Hindu tradition. The "fire bath" isn't an actual bath, of course, but it mimics the act of bathing because it refers to cleansing your body. The bath actually does much more than that; it expunges the aura of negativity and impurities and "eats away" at the Evil Eye the same way flames eat up dry logs.

You will need:

- Two white taper candles

- Two candleholders

To do this spell, you will need to be alone, in a private space, for at least fifteen minutes. When you're ready, set the candleholders on a hard surface that is level or almost level with your midsection (a table or kitchen counter work best). Stand still. Hold one of the taper candles in your hands and take three deep breaths. Slowly and gently roll the candle over your body. Start at your head and work downward, ending at your feet. Place the candle in one of the holders.

Repeat the process with the second candle.

Light both candles and then stand in front of them while keeping your distance. (You shouldn't be close enough to actually feel the heat of the candles). Raise your arms out to your sides and close your eyes. Spend at least five to seven minutes concentrating on what you want the fire to burn out of your life.

When you're done, turn around fully so that your back is now facing the candles. Close your eyes and concentrate on what it is that you want to regenerate or "spark up" in your life. Is it peace of mind? Improved health? Think about how the Eye has impacted your life. If it's financially, for example, concentrate on fixing that condition. If a relationship is being shaken up, concentrate on restoring love and balance to your life.

When you're done, extinguish the candles. Repeat the spell for at least three consecutive nights.

The Magic Cup

I learned this spell when I was a kid, and I still use it if I think I'm being hit with a particularly persistent Evil Eye. This is also a great spell to use if a child has fallen victim to the Eye; constructing the spell is fun and creative, and a child doesn't necessarily have to know they're crafting a magical tool for healing.

You will need:

- A white cup (a ceramic cup is best, but a plain white paper cup will also work)

- Blue marker

- Black marker

- The Sun tarot card

- Clean cloth (a thick square of paper towel will also work)

- Rubber band

This spell is best done on a bright, sunny day. On one side of the cup, draw a nazar, using the blue marker to make the circles and the black marker to make the dot in the center. On the opposite side of the cup, draw an eye. In between the two symbols, write your name or the name of the afflicted individual. Fill the cup with water. Seal the rim with the cloth and rubber band. Place

The Sun tarot card on a windowsill, image up, and then place the cup on top of the card. Leave the cup there for an hour and let it soak up the sun's magical, healing, and protective energy. Then remove the cloth and drink up!

Spell for Fertility

A happy couple or a happy woman who wants to conceive is a target for envy. If you, a loved one, or a couple you know is having trouble getting pregnant, the Evil Eye may very well be the cause.

You will need:

- Three cashews

- A red drawstring pouch

- Two strands of red ribbon or cord

- One piece of red coral

Ideally, this spell should be performed at the time of the new moon. Begin with the ribbons or cords; bind them by tying a knot at one end. As you braid the two strands together, chant the following:

The horses galloped toward the rising sun, the horses galloped toward the rising sun.

Place the braid and the piece of red coral in the pouch and tie the drawstrings together. Put the pouch on your nightstand and wait twenty-four hours. Then, take the pouch, untie the draw-string, and place the three cashews inside it. As you do, chant the following:

The horses galloped toward the rising sun, and a full day later, the horses and sun forever became one.

Retie the drawstrings to close the pouch. Now, moisten the tip of the thumb of your dominant hand and with that thumb gently draw a circle over the outside of the pouch. If you have a partner, instruct them to do the same. This seals the spell.

Hang the pouch above your bed or set it on your nightstand.

Spells for Renewed Sexual Potency

When the Evil Eye strikes men, it frequently hits below the waist. Sudden performance problems—if not downright impotence— are a common symptom and sign. If the Eye's presence is confirmed and you or a man you know is experiencing an unexplained bout of erectile dysfunction, perform the following spells.

For the first spell, make an offering to Sant'Ippazio. Venerated by both the Roman Catholic and Eastern Orthodox Churches, the cult of Sant'Ippazio is especially popular in Southern Italy. As the story goes, Sant'Ippazio suffered a blow to his lower abdominal region and developed an inguinal hernia, which caused his penis to resemble a carrot. He is petitioned for matters regarding impotence, erectile dysfunction, and male infertility. Though Catholic in origin, men of every faith (and no particular faith at all) have invoked the aid of Sant'Ippazio.

You will need:

• One red or purple carrot

• A glass of wine

• A trowel or large spoon

Go outside and find a quiet woodsy place. With the trowel, dig a small hole, hollowing it out as much as possible. Take the carrot in one hand and the glass of wine in the other. As you pour the wine over the tip of the carrot, recite the following:

From the vine, blood flows like wine, Sant'Ippazio mortal, Sant'Ippazio divine, make whole again this body of mine.

When the wine has been emptied over the tip of the carrot, place the carrot into the hole in the ground—make sure it's point up, facing the sky. Cover the hole with soil. Turn around and walk away without looking back.

(Note: If you can't perform this spell in your own backyard, try a park or green space. If you're far from either, get a tall jug or pitcher and fill it with dirt or soil, into which you will deposit the carrot.)

For the second spell, print a picture of the mano cornuto on a piece of paper. Alternatively, you can draw the symbol yourself. In either case, make sure it's in color—bright blood red. When the ink has dried, place the picture under your mattress with the points facing up (toward where you rest your head). Replace the picture every three months.

Three and the Eye Can't See

Much like the "Five in Your Eye" technique mentioned on page 25, the following spell is simple, quick, and powerful. It requires nothing more than your own dominant hand, and it can be performed anywhere. If you feel that you are suffering from the Eye's negative energy but don't have the ability to perform a diagnosing ritual, find a quiet place—an office or cubical, even a bathroom—and do the following:

Make a fist with your right hand. Raise your fist above your head. As you extend your thumb say: *One—I find you.* Extend your index finger and say: *Two—I bind you.* Extend your middle finger and say: *Three—I blind you.*

Lower your hand, shake it loose, and walk away from where you were standing without looking back.

SMOKING THE EYE AWAY

In many cultures, the use of smoke is sacred; it is used to cleanse the energy fields that surround our homes, cars, offices, and various objects. That same energy also exists *within* places and objects. Your home and car are perfect examples. There's energy around the circumference of your house or car, but there's also energy contained within its walls and doors.

This is also true of our bodies. If you stretch your arms out and look at your hands, you might think your body ends where your fingertips do. But that's not true. Energy emanates from our bodies and extends beyond our flesh. This is called the auric field, and like any other field, it can get polluted. The practice of ritual cleansing literally cleans and renews energy, which in turn reinforces our own physical and mental energy levels. The technique of using smoke to do this is ancient, powerful, and practical. It is not rooted in any one faith or culture but belongs to the wisdom of Earth itself.

Incense sticks aren't the only way to create sacred smoke. It can be done using herbs, seeds, botanicals, and wood. You will need an incense burner or fire-proof plate and some charcoal disks.

Herbs and Plants

Basil: Burn basil leaves when you feel a relationship is being targeted by the Evil Eye. If a romantic relationship is in trouble, make sure to waft the smoke in the bedroom of your home. If you don't live with your partner, cleanse any gifts you have received.

Bay Laurel: Burning a bay leaf creates a pungent smell, but its power to drive away negativity is tremendous. It's especially good when moving into a new home.

Garlic: It's an herb, it's a spice, it's a vegetable—whatever the case, garlic is immeasurably potent. Burning a clove of garlic has the power of a sword. That said, I use garlic cautiously because it's so powerful. If you feel the Eye is especially strong and its effects are lasting for days, definitely burn garlic. I know a witch who uses sautéed garlic as incense, carrying a pan through every room of her house. A special note: In parts of Southern Italy, a mixture of garlic, rue, and rosemary is used to summon spirits and keep the dead close.

Lavender: Burn lavender when the Eye has caused a physical ailment. If a doctor has ruled out a medical condition and you're still feeling lethargic or "out of it," lavender smoke will cleanse the maligned energy from your body and auric field.

Mint: Burn mint whenever the Eye has hit you on the financial front. Waft its smoke around your wallet, purse, and financial statements.

Rosemary: You can burn rosemary for so many reasons—it's truly a mystical herb. It's among my top three favorites, and I usually burn rosemary before performing a ritual or spell, and before and after I do tarot and Evil Eye readings. Let its smoke calm you when the Eye has caused anxiety.

Rue: Common rue, also known as the herb of grace, is probably the most frequently used herb when it comes to magic. Burning it will cleanse all kinds of negativity.

Syrian Rue: Most of the herbs and plants on this list are common. If you haven't already used them, you can find them easily.

That said, I'm making a special note here about Syrian rue because it is (1) often confused with common rue and (2) Syrian rue is especially powerful when it comes to combating the Evil Eye. Syrian rue is common in the Middle East and North Africa, where it's called *harmal*. When the plant is dried, its seeds (*esfand*) can be removed and burned. Its smoke is fragrant and does double duty by breaking the Eye's curse and entirely stopping someone from casting a malicious glance. Drop a few esfand seeds on lit charcoal. Cleanse yourself by carefully lifting the plate and moving it from your head to your feet. You can also waft it in the corners and doorways of your home or office, or toss a handful of seeds into a fire. The smoke is a powerful agent for neutralizing harm. (The seeds pop, so don't be alarmed when you hear them doing so!)

Woods

Cedar: Used for all kinds of purification, cedar is especially good for keeping unwanted guests away from your home. Use the smoke in your front doorway to clear away the Eye and to deflect envious glances.

Juniper: Sacred to the god Apollo and the goddess Astarte, juniper wood is another "double duty agent": its smoke clears negativity while also attracting good fortune.

Palo Santo: Much has been written about Palo Santo, and its benefits are numerous. I find Palo Santo especially powerful when the Evil Eye is emanating from a constant source—a person you see and/or engage with regularly, be it at work or in your neighborhood. Its pungent smoke never weakens and will burn away envy and resentment with speed.

Pine: Commonly thought of around Christmas, pine can (and should) be burned all year long. It is especially effective after having hosted a group of people in your home. The Evil Eye gains strength in groups, and the pine smoke will vanquish these harmful energies.

Sandalwood: If you've ever been to a religious ritual, you've probably experienced the scent of sandalwood. It has strong protection properties and is excellent to burn for all matters relating to business. Burn it in your office, your shop, your studio—any place that is linked to your livelihood—to keep the Eye away.

THE EVIL EYE PANTRY

In the home of every magical practitioner is what I like to think of as an "enchanted" alcove. Actually, it doesn't have to be an alcove at all. A pantry can be a closet shelf or a specially appointed drawer; it can even be a windowsill upon which jars and other accoutrements are stored and arranged.

So why do you need a space dedicated to your Evil Eye practice? Because Evil Eye magic is distinct. It's ubiquitous but also deeply intimate. This is the magic that heals your mind and body, protects your home and children and pets, and ensures that your most meaningful events run smoothly. As you've learned, that takes knowledge, skill, effort . . . and ingredients! Below is what I keep in my own Evil Eye pantry and I highly recommend that you store at least a few of the items on this list in your home.

A note: you don't have to have a separate bottle of olive oil reserved solely for diagnosing the Eye; take the oil that you use for cooking and carefully pour some of it into a jar or smaller bottle, and keep *that* one in your Evil Eye pantry. The same rules apply for the garlic, salt, and other ingredients. Folk magic comes from people who didn't have lots of money or an abundance of supplies, and their magic was powerful—so powerful that it has been dutifully passed down from generation to generation. The only item that I *do* recommend you purchase new is the bowl you will fill with water and use to detect the Eye; it doesn't have to be expensive, but tuck it away and don't let anyone else make use of it.

Basil: People tend to associate basil with love—it does, in fact, work for love spells—but this beautiful herb packs a punch when it comes to protection. To cleanse your home of negativity, brew a cup of basil tea, mix it with a gallon of water, and use as a floor wash. Want to ward against the Evil Eye on your wedding day? Make an herbal amulet: spit into a basil leaf, roll it toward you, and tie it up with a blue string; at the end of the day, burn the leaf.

Bay leaves: This herb's list of magical properties is extensive, and it can be used in numerous ways to combat negativity. To dream of the person who gave you the Eye, spit on a bay leaf, place it in a drawstring pouch, and sleep with it under your pillow; the person's identity will be revealed within three nights. Do you know who gave you the Evil Eye? If so, write their name on a bay leaf and burn it. If you know who gave you the Eye and you want to return the curse to them, write their name on a bay leaf and tape the bay leaf facedown to a picture of the offender. If you don't have a picture, tape the bay leaf with their name on it (again facedown) to a small mirror. Is the Eye hurting your financial life? If so, wrap a single dollar bill around two bay leaves and place the charm in your purse or wallet.

Candles: The most popular magical tool, candles serve many purposes. In working spells and rituals, they are invaluable, but sometimes just lighting a candle and meditating or praying before it can provide answers to a confusing or bothersome situation. A candle's color figures into a spell's intention, but when it comes to magic, not everything is about spells. If you want to keep matters simple, store a few white chime candles in your pantry and light one when you feel moved to do so. Some practitioners light a white candle whenever they diagnose the Eye because the element of fire is cleansing.

Chili peppers: Fresh *red* chili peppers hung in any room will burn away the Evil Eye. This natural charm will also expose secrets, either yours or those of anyone else who lives in the home. A common Hindu remedy to deflect negativity and attract good luck calls for cinching together seven *green* chili peppers and a lemon and then hanging the charm in the kitchen; replace it every seven days.

Cloves: Because of their phallic shape, cloves are natural amulets and possess a wide range of protective properties. According to folklore, exorcists carried cloves to help them chase away the devil. The easiest way to use cloves is by placing nine of them in a pouch and then either carrying the pouch or hanging it in your home. To ward against the Evil Eye at work, tape a single clove—with the point facing away from you—under your desk. A quick spell to remove the Eye: gently push a clove into a blue chime candle and let it burn out completely.

Dill: Common symptoms of the Evil Eye include frequent nightmares and insomnia. A remedy: place a clove of garlic and dill in a glass of water and then leave the glass under the bed. Dill held in the palm of your hand will act as a quick herbal amulet. Add dill or dill seeds to a pouch to ward away the Eye. Associated with the sacral chakra, dill is an effective ingredient in spells and magic aimed at curing impotence and infertility.

Garlic: It wards away negativity of all kinds, but when ingested, used for spellwork, or placed in a specific area for a limited amount of time, it will banish and bust the Evil Eye. Hanging braided garlic in the kitchen window will repel burglars. Pay attention to who's around you if a section of braided garlic breaks off or drops, as this is a sign of deception in your midst.

Lemons: Citrus is the magic of both the sun and moon. When cut and placed on a plate, lemon halves will absorb negative energy; when placed in a spray bottle with water, the mixture becomes a fragrant cleanser. Add lemon juice to a bath to expel the Evil Eye. A quick warding spell to use when you get sudden, unwanted company: cut a lemon in half and place both pieces on a plate with the inside facing outward, then sprinkle with salt.

Liquore Strega: Practitioners of Italian folk magic tend to have a particular fondness for this herbal alcoholic beverage. Legend has it that the "witch liquor" mixture was originally brewed in 1860 in Benevento, Italy, as a love potion. Today it is mostly enjoyed as a *digestif* after meals. The liqueur gets its unique yellowish color from saffron, an herb with an ancient and rich history; used medicinally to aid in the healing of numerous illnesses, saffron also has tremendous protective qualities. A simple cure for the Evil Eye: drop a blue bead in a shot glass filled with Strega Liquore and leave it at your bedside. To ward away the Eye, anoint the doorframes of your home with the liqueur.

Matches: The old-fashioned wooden stick "kitchen matches" are of great use to practitioners of Evil Eye magic. See pages 137 and 176 for rituals involving matches, but a match can also be used when you need a quick remedy and either aren't home or don't have time to do a more in-depth working. When you feel surrounded by the Eye's negative energy, light a match and whisper a prayer or protective verse as the match burns down. Fire cleanses.

Olive oil: The magical uses for olive oil could fill a book. When it comes to Evil Eye magic, oil becomes a tool for divination.

You can also use it to anoint yourself or items you wish to bless. Add a sliver of garlic to a tablespoon of olive oil and then use the oil to bless your car by dabbing each door and window with it.

Parsley: When the Evil Eye attacks your marriage or current relationship, this is the herb to reach for. Tie a bunch of parsley with a red ribbon and sweep it over your bed at dusk. Place dried parsley in a red pouch and slip it under your mattress. Brides and grooms should carry a blue pouch filled with parsley as close to their waists as possible to ward against sexual dysfunction. For especially strong and powerful parsley, plant some on Good Friday.

Ribbon, string, and cord: Every so often we need to tie things up, or bind them, so a bulk of ribbon, string, or cord is important to have on hand. Knot and cord magic is powerful and practical; you can perform it anywhere. Ribbon is also an excellent magical tool because it can be charged or infused with energy and then displayed as a decoration. Blue and red are the most common colors for Evil Eye magic.

Rosemary: According to legend, the Virgin Mary dropped her cloak onto a rosemary bush as she fled Egypt, thereby gracing the herb with magical properties. When planted around a house, it acts as a shield. Burn rosemary after a large event or if you think even a single guest at your dinner table was emitting envious vibes. The old saying *rosemary for remembrance* applies when packing rosemary into a small pouch or charm bag and wearing it as an amulet—it is said that the Evil Eye remembers the powers of rosemary and thus stays clear of it.

Rue: In his book *The Witching Herbs*, master gardener and magician Harold Roth calls rue "the subtle warrior"—and for good reason. It's an immensely powerful herb. Roth writes: "it is used to keep away demons (*jnun*) and frequently turns up in rituals meant to purify an area of such entities, as well as in protective charms to keep them away. It is also worn as a protective amulet, since it keeps off the Evil Eye." Brew a tea of rue and add it to your bath. Affix a sprig of it to your front door and replace it every few days. When it comes to protection and cleansing, rue wears the crown. However, it's important to remember that pregnant women or nursing mothers should not use rue.

Salt: A staple of protection and healing, salt can be used for warding in the simplest ways. A handful of salt dropped into a velvet or satin pouch makes for a powerful talisman. Sprinkling salt in the corners of a room absorbs bad juju.

CHAPTER SIX

HOW TO CAST THE EVIL EYE

It sounds counterintuitive. It might even sound outlandish. After spending a whole book learning about the dangers of the Evil Eye and the ways in which to ward and remove it, why would you want to learn how to cast it? That's probably your first question. You likely have several others, among them: *Won't the Eye's curse boomerang back? Isn't it unethical to look at someone and wish them harm? How much harm can I actually do?* These are all valid queries, and, as you approach them with an open mind, the answers might surprise you; they might even redefine your ideas about self-defense and the power inherent in your own mind/body connection.

Learning how to cast the Evil Eye is a many-layered topic. The first is all about protection—your own, and that of your loved ones, your home, and your possessions. The warding techniques and spells in previous chapters will help you keep negativity at bay and expel it from your life completely, but knowing how to use your own eyes and energy in a threatening situation is the ultimate form of self-defense.

Picture yourself in the following scenario. You're sitting in a restaurant minding your own business when you glance up from your plate and realize that someone is staring at you. Not a stranger, but a neighbor who has made her dislike of you known in the past. A couple of months ago, she snickered when she walked past your house. Last week, the mailman told you that Nasty Neighbor made comments about the landscaping project currently underway in your yard. She even used a few distasteful words when describing you. The secret is out: you have an enemy. Now that enemy is standing a few feet away from you, and she's being brazen in her attempts to intimidate you. Maybe she's even trying to curse you by wishing that your house and its noisy landscaping project burn to the ground. Her actions—even if they appear to be nothing more than prolonged stares and muttering—are nonetheless disturbing.

Let's pause here for a moment. This anecdote has two possible endings. If you're not the confrontational type, you'll probably rush through what's left of your meal, pay the bill, and hurry to your car. Hours later, in the comfort of your own home, you'll feel rattled by the incident. Your mind will keep going back to Nasty Neighbor's face and the blatant hatred that had been gleaming in her eyes. In your mounting panic, you might start wondering how far the neighbor will go in her campaign to scare you. You spend most of the night awake in bed, picturing the woman walking toward your back door in the dark. In the days that follow, you feel your stomach clench whenever you see said neighbor. Every one of her stares is like an electric shock to your spine. It's not a good thing.

But there could easily be another ending to this tale. Think back to the moment you looked up from your plate in the restaurant and saw your neighbor staring you down. As someone who's well educated about the Evil Eye, you know exactly what she's trying to do. Instead of pretending to ignore her while telling yourself that she and her immature ways aren't worth your time—instead of making the mistake of "turning the other cheek"—you set down your fork, sit back, and meet her stare head-on. You meet her stare with such stealth and precision that the world around you shivers completely out of focus. It's no longer a matter of two people staring each other down. Your neighbor has become a clear and present danger, and your own eyes are the weapons that will stop her attack and send it hurtling back to its point of origin.

Seconds later you recognize your success. Your neighbor glances away quickly or gives a little start—not because she's been frightened by the look in your eyes, but because she actually *felt* the energy emerging from them. She felt the energy as surely as she would have felt a needle prick her skin.

This is not wishful thinking on your part, nor is it the theory of extramission at work. It's simply the Evil Eye being cast through your own knowledge, effort, and skill. Soon your neighbor will see the manifestation of the Eye in her own life; the degree of chaos she experiences depends on the degree of intensity with which you chose to unleash your own quiet curse. Without a doubt, your neighbor will stop harassing you.

This is an example of how learning to cast the Evil Eye can benefit you. Instead of becoming a victim, you retaliated and averted a bomb—a bomb that someone else was willing to drop into the middle of your life. In such situations, is there really any sense in looking away or trying to "be the bigger/better person"?

What would you do if a strange guy at your office stared at you suggestively every time you stood and waited for the elevator? His look might not be particularly threatening; in fact, he might think he's paying you a compliment. But the weight of his stare conveys to you a very different message, a message that unsettles you. Giving him the Eye will change the way he looks at you because he very likely won't look at you again. By using the proper method, you can send a warning through a glance—not a hollow warning that merely illustrates your distaste or annoyance, but a warning that will materialize in real time.

There's a good chance you might not want to admit that these scenarios resonate with you, stirring up thoughts and feelings that fester in the darkest corners of your psyche. Rarely do we admit our all too human desires to exact revenge or inflict harm on those who have wronged us. But that's exactly what the Evil Eye can do.

I've given you examples that fall under the heading of "self-defense," but there are other circumstances wherein giving the Eye is wholly appropriate. Have you ever experienced genuine cruelty? I'm not referring to the mean boss who denied your vacation request or the acquaintance gossiping about how awful your new haircut is. I'm referring to the boss who purposely sabotaged your promotion and the acquaintance trying to break up your marriage through a series of calculated lies. In both cases, the threat might not introduce itself as overtly as a glance—which, in my opinion, makes the danger all the more palpable—so you may have to take matters into your own hands and cast the first look. Ensnare the boss or acquaintance in your ocular net and launch the Eye into their lives. Even if the damage to your own life is done, you get the satisfaction—yes, you read that correctly—of seeing justice served. This doesn't make you a bad person, nor does it mean you revel in evil, malice, or the act of inflicting pain on others. If you draw any pleasure from watching justice unfold, raise your hand and repeat after me: *"I'm human."*

Is there an "ethical" component to magic? Yes, and the meaning of the word *ethical* depends entirely on your own definitions of protection, defense, and justice. But I don't think I'm going out on a limb when I state that most people have experienced the soul-piercing pain of injustice and then wished, yearned, and hungered to see the source—i.e., the person or persons—of that injustice pay for their wrongdoing. Thankfully, the majority of people don't take the law into their own hands. There's a big difference between self-defense and vigilantism, and magical practice teaches the practitioner that lesson right away. If you think you're going to strut around giving every person in your midst the Evil Eye simply because you know how to do it or because you think you're all-powerful, prepare yourself for dark times. It doesn't work like that.

I'm not trying to scare you with notions of payback. I'm simply stating that any form of magic requires a certain level of maturity from the practitioner. You have to examine a situation as dispassionately and with as little emotion as possible before deciding to unleash the fury of the Evil Eye—or any curse, for that matter.

Whenever I tell people that I practice Italian folk magic, I'm almost always asked if curses are real. My answer is an unequivocal "Yes." Anyone who researches the history of folk magic traditions will find evidence of various curses and hexes among the populations from which those traditions arose. Such evidence doesn't delineate an entire group of individuals so much as it illuminates the reality of human nature. Folk magic and witchcraft are mirrors of truth; each is a reflection of the natural world and our place within it. The instinct to defend and fight back is primal, not fleeting. When witches and other magical practitioners cast justified curses, we are restoring balance to our own lives and to the cycle of life itself.

THE JETTATORE

In Italian folklore, there are people who are born with an extremely strong ability to cast the Evil Eye. Called a *jettatore*, this individual—usually a man—can bring about misfortune, misery, danger, and sometimes death with his stare. It's important to note that a jettatore doesn't always create chaos intentionally. His power can't be controlled, and bad luck always seems to follow in his wake. In parts of Sicily and Southern Italy, the jettatore is still greatly feared.

CASTING THE EYE

Learning how to cast the Evil Eye rests upon a single principle: *know thyself.* Sound familiar? Of course it does, but there's a big difference between knowing yourself and knowing yourself as a *magical practitioner.*

I stated earlier that learning how to detect and cure the Evil Eye is serious business, and it is; you're working with energy, some of it negative, and it can impact your life. That bit of advice is doubled when you learn how to cast the Eye. Why? Because you're using your *own* energy to essentially ward off an attack, and you're using your body to expend that energy. If you've experienced this before, you know how exhausting it can be. If you're new to it, prepare to be drained, at least initially.

Knowing yourself as a magical practitioner means accepting that certain things might happen once you've become proficient at casting the Evil Eye. No, you won't attract demons or bad luck into your life, but you will experience episodes when you suddenly feel energy coursing through your body. You may also have vivid dreams. Above all, you will start seeing evidence of your work.

You might see your target trip or cry. You might hear that they are suddenly going through a rough time. How will that make you feel? Don't answer that question right now. Imagine it unfolding and be honest with yourself about the emotions a scenario like this brings up in you.

TRIGGER EMOTION: HOW IT HAPPENS

The nucleus of successfully casting the Evil Eye is the emotional energy that essentially creates the curse. This is where the work gets a little ugly. Think back to a time in your life when you felt deeply wounded by injustice. Who mistreated you, manipulated you, or set you up for failure? The person or persons who victimized you likely waltzed out of your life without a second glance and left you alone to pick up the pieces. Remember how you screamed at your bedroom wall while imagining the person standing in front of you? If you didn't do that, you definitely imagined telling them off. The point I'm trying to make is that you experienced raw emotion—so much anger that just thinking back on the whole episode causes that anger to flare up again.

Are you feeling it now? If so, sit with it for a while. Make friends with it, but don't mitigate its power. You need to feel that energy without letting the energy wreck you the way it did the first time. Some people, upon sensing that emotion a second time, perform a visualization exercise in which they "sculpt" the energy into a specific shape—a shape that makes them feel empowered.

What shape or symbol makes you feel empowered? A sword? An arrow? A spider's web? A candle with an insanely sharp flame? I think you get the picture.

The initial step in learning how to cast the Evil Eye is getting in touch with this raw emotion and cultivating it so that it will work for you in a new way. The first time around, it likely dominated you. This time around, you're the one in control, and *you* get to dominate *it*.

THE SHIELD

A staple in magical practice, drawing a shield around yourself creates a barrier of energy that wards away negativity while keeping your own energy grounded and sharp. In general, it's a good idea to place a protection shield around yourself every day, but the one you'll be using here is specifically for those times when you might need to cast the Evil Eye. The process is simple but requires focus.

To draw your shield, follow these steps: Go to a quiet place where you won't be disturbed. It doesn't matter if you retreat to your bedroom, your car, or a public restroom. All you need is one solid minute. Take three deep breaths. Close your eyes and, beginning at the top of your head, mentally draw a circle around your body. Visualize a blue light forming around your head, then traveling down to cover the points at your shoulders, arms, waist, feet and then up the opposite side of your body.

When the circle meets and closes above your head, intone a word that signals closure to you. You can say "Amen" or "So mote it be." You can also say "Done" if that resonates with you.

Now, draw the shape of an eye—a large eye—directly over your abdomen. Picture the shape of an almond, and then draw a circle within it. The eye does not have an eyelid or lashes. It's an open eye because its energy is all-seeing and aware. Repeat your chosen word of closure and open your eyes.

That's all there is to it. Practice drawing the ocular shield around yourself until it feels like second nature. Soon you'll be able to do it in less than a minute. Eventually you'll be able to do it in seconds because your mind will automatically drop the eye into place before you start to psychically draw it.

THE METHODS

Eye-to-Eye

The most effective way to cast the Evil Eye is in person, face-to-face. The following steps might seem like a lot, but you have to read through the list and memorize the steps before actually trying to cast the Eye on someone. Think of it as a rehearsal—you can't go on stage until you've learned your lines and are comfortable in the scene.

You'll know you're ready once the steps feel fluid. You won't even have to mentally count them down or actively think about them. The steps will collapse into a quick sequence and come together in just a few seconds.

With your target in eyeshot, ground and center yourself by taking three deep breaths. If you're sitting, relax your shoulders. If you're standing, tighten your core muscles.

Look down without moving your head. Focus on your right shoe or something on the floor. Raise your shield.

What's your trigger emotion? Unleash it. Picture it as a raging river, a python uncoiling, an arrow cutting through the air at breakneck speed. Feel the emotion. Feel it filling your solar plexus. Feel it *thudding, pulsing, rushing, roaring.* Contain the energy for only two or three seconds. Count down the seconds if it helps.

Now guide the energy up to your eyes. You can do this by directing it through your spinal column and then straight through your head and to your eyes, or you can guide the energy up the front of your body. Go with the method that makes you feel most comfortable. Remember: it's energy, and it changes form according to how you direct it. You must be able to feel the energy "humming" around your eyes. Sometimes you'll feel it in your nasal cavity or at your temples.

Look up. If your target is facing you, stare directly into their eyes and eject the energy out of your own eyes in one fast shot without blinking. As you do this, make the mano fica gesture with your right hand, but keep your hand concealed, either in a pocket or down at your side. Look down again and blink.

The first few times you attempt to cast the Eye, you'll come away from the experience feeling drained. The best remedy for this is simply to relax. If you can leave the area, do so, and always do it without looking back.

The Picture

It's not always possible to meet your target in person. They may live far away, or you might have different schedules. Even so, it's possible to cast the Eye without being physically in their presence.

Obtain a picture of your target; it doesn't have to be head-shot-quality, but you must be able to see their eyes clearly. Once you have the picture, hold it in front of you and use the same steps as detailed above. Bring up the trigger emotion, focus on the target's eyes, and eject your energy out of your own eyes. Make the mano fica gesture as you do this.

After looking away and blinking, return your gaze to the picture. Lick the thumb of your right hand and draw a short line— from top to bottom—over the target's left eye. Then lick the thumb or left hand and draw the same line over the target's right eye.

Quickly turn the picture over. Don't look at it again.

EPILOGUE

If ever there was a time to mine Evil Eye traditions and magic, it's now. Knowing how to detect and cure the quiet curse will undoubtedly improve your life and the lives of your loved ones, but being "armed" with this knowledge also grants you agency in uncertain times. Frightening global headlines only tell half of the story. When we observe our immediate environments, what we often see in others is a plethora of harsh emotions: anger, resentment, jealousy, avarice. Coveting has become a way of life for many. Your colleague's paycheck is bigger, your neighbor's house is newer, your best friend's private life is more fulfilling. Greed seems unending.

In the midst of it all, we yearn for something that we can't quite name. Stability? Serenity? Security? Evil Eye amulets are everywhere—television, magazines, Instagram feeds. Why? A nazar is much more than a fashion statement. What's fueling the interest in new (but very old) ways to feel safe? At the heart of our longing is a desire to see the unseen, to be able to recognize a threat before it becomes a danger. Thankfully, magic grants us that very ability. When you become *aware* of the Evil Eye, you open up your inner eye—the instinct to examine your surroundings and the people in it. As you acknowledge that instinct, you also sharpen it, and your inner eye begins "to see" in the metaphysical sense. This is not vision, but intuition. The inner eye "sees" in terms of gut feelings. When you recognize that the bad luck isn't random, when you catch in the glance of another a dagger of envy, you are taking control of the very circumstances you have been taught to believe are uncontrollable. This is magic. More specifically, this is Evil Eye magic.

The rituals, prayers, and practices that are now in your hands comprise traditions that are thousands of years old. They anchor us among our ancestors and strengthen us as part of a global community of practitioners. Is there anything more powerful in an age of social isolation and societal fragmentation? Is there anything more reassuring than knowing you have the ability to change the course of your own life and the lives of those around you?

Like the Evil Eye itself, the magic and methods in this book are timeless. And now the magic is yours. May you always possess the sacred vision to heal, protect, and transform.

APPENDIX

THE EVIL EYE AROUND
THE WORLD

It has many different names and is alive in many different places, but the Evil Eye transcends both language and location. The following list of names for the Eye—by no means exhaustive—is further evidence of its ubiquity.

Albanian: *syri i keq* or *syni keq*
Arabic: *al-ayn* or *hasad*
Armenian: *char atchk* or *char achq*
Corsican: *l'Ochju* or *ochju*
Dutch: *het boze oog*
French: *le mauvais œil*
Galician: *meigallo*
German: *böser Blick*
Greek: *matiasma* or *mati*
Hebrew: *ayin hara*
Hindi (and other languages of South Asia): *nazar*
Hungarian: *gonosz szem* and also *rossz nezes* or *szemveres*

Irish: *drochshúil* or *an droch shuil*
Italian: *malocchio*
Japanese: *jashi*
Lithuanian: *pikta akis*
Malay: *mata jahat*
Maltese: *l-għajn, sahta,* or *seher*
Persian: *chesm, cheshmeh shoor, chashm zakhm,* or *nazar*
Polish: *złe oko* or *złe spojrzenie*
Portuguese: *mau olhado* or *olho gordo*
Romanian: *deochi*
Slovak: *z očí* or *oci pocaric*
Somali: *ilaaco*
Spanish: *mal de ojo*
Trinidadian Creole: *maljo*
Turkish: *kem göz* or *nazar*
Yiddish: *ayin hora*

BIBLIOGRAPHY

Alvarado, Denise. *The Magic of Marie Laveau: Embracing the Spiritual Legacy of the Voodoo Queen of New Orleans*. Massachusetts: Weiser Books, 2020.

———. *Witch Queens, Voodoo Spirits & Hoodoo Saints: A Guide to Magical New Orleans*. Massachusetts: Weiser Books, 2022.

Armstrong, Karen. *The Great Transformation: The Beginning of Our Religion Traditions*. New York: Anchor Books, 2007.

Bird, Stephanie Rose. *Sticks, Stones, Roots & Bones: Hoodoo, Mojo & Conjuring with Herbs*. Minnesota: Llewellyn Publications, 2004.

Blackthorn, Amy. *Sacred Smoke: Clear Away Negative Energies and Purify Body, Mind and Spirit*. Massachusetts: Weiser Books, 2019.

Bohak, Gideon. *Ancient Jewish Magic: A History*. New York: Cambridge University Press, 2011.

Cohen, Deatra. *Ashkenazi Herbalism: Rediscovering the Herbal Traditions of Eastern European Jews*. California: North Atlantic Books, 2021.

Cross, J. Allen. *American Brujeria: Modern Mexican American Folk Magic.* Massachusetts: Weiser Books, 2021.

Daugherty, Martin J. *Hindu Myths: From Cosmology to Gods, Demons and Magic.* London: Amber Books, 2020.

de Martino, Ernesto. Dorothy Louise Zinn, translator. *Magic: A Theory from the South.* London: HAU Books, 2015.

Dennis, Geoffrey W. *The Encyclopedia of Jewish Myth, Magic & Superstition.* Minnesota: Llewellyn Publications, 2016.

Doostdar, Alireza. *The Iranian Metaphysicals: Explorations in Science, Islam and the Uncanny.* New Jersey: Princeton University Press, 2018.

Dundes, Alan (Ed.). *The Evil Eye: A Casebook.* Wisconsin: The University of Wisconsin Press, 1981.

Elliott, John H. *Beware the Evil Eye: The Evil Eye in the Bible and the Ancient World: Volume 2: Greece and Rome.* Oregon: Cascade Books, 2016.

———. *Beware the Evil Eye Volume 3: The Evil Eye in the Bible and the Ancient World.* Oregon: Cascade Books, 2016.

Elworthy, Frederick Thomas. *The Evil Eye: The Classic Account of an Ancient Superstition.* New York: Dover Publications, 2004.

Fahrun, Mary-Grace. *Italian Folk Magic: Rue's Kitchen Witchery.* Massachusetts: Weiser Books, 2018.

Faraone, Christopher A. *The Transformation of Greek Amulets in Roman Imperial Times.* Pennsylvania: University of Pennsylvania Press, 2018.

Grimassi, Raven. *Italian Witchcraft: The Old Religion of Southern Europe.* Minnesota: Llewellyn Publications, 2000.

Hutcheson, Cory Thomas. *New World Witchery: A Trove of North American Folk Magic.* Minnesota: Llewellyn Publications, 2021.

Illes, Judika. *Encyclopedia of 5,000 Spells: The Ultimate Reference Book for the Magical Arts.* New York: HarperOne, 2008.

————. *Encyclopedia of Spirits: The Ultimate Guide to the Magic of Fairies, Genies, Demons, Ghosts, Gods & Goddesses.* New York: HarperOne, 2009.

————. *Encyclopedia of Mystics, Saints & Sages: A Guide to Asking for Protection, Wealth, Happiness, and Everything Else!* New York: HarperOne, 2011.

————. *Encyclopedia of Witchcraft: The Complete A-Z for the Entire Magical World.* New York: HarperOne, 2014.

Knight, Michael Muhammad. *Magic in Islam.* New York: Tarcher-Perigee, 2016.

Magliocco, Sabina. *Witching Culture: Folklore and Neo-Paganism in America.* Pennsylvania: University of Pennsylvania Press, 2004.

Martello, Leo Louis. *Witchcraft: The Old Religion.* New York: Citadel Press, 1991.

————. *Weird Ways of Witchcraft.* Massachusetts: Weiser Books, 2011

Mastros, Sara L. *The Big Book of Magical Incense.* Massachusetts: Weiser Books, 2021.

Mickaharic, Draja. *Spiritual Cleansings: A Handbook for Psychic Protection.* Massachusetts: Weiser Books, 2022.

Miller, Jason. *Protection & Reversal Magic: A Witch's Defense Manual.* Massachusetts: Weiser Books, 2006.

Mitchell, Stephen. *Bhagavad Gita: A New Translation.* New York: Harmony Books, 2002.

Penczak, Christopher. *The Witch's Shield: Protection Magic and Psychic Self-Defense.* Minnesota: Llewellyn Publications, 2004.

Roth, Harold. *The Witching Herbs: 13 Essential Plants and Herbs for Your Magical Garden.* Massachusetts: Weiser Books, 2017.

Sheldrake, Rupert. *The Sense of Being Stared At: And Other Unexplained Powers of Human Minds.* Rochester, Vermont; Toronto Canada: Park Street Press, 2013.

Trachtenberg, Joshua. *Jewish Magic and Superstition: A Study in Folk Religion.* Connecticut: Martino Publishing.

ACADEMIC PAPERS

Bohigian, George H. "The History of the Evil Eye and Its Influence on Ophthalmology, Medicine and Social Customs." 1997. Kluwer Academic Publishers, 91–100.

Davis, Eli. "The Psalms in Hebrew Medical Amulets." 1992. *Vetus Testamentum*, Vol. 42, 173–178.

Finneran, Niall. "Ethiopian Evil Eye Belief and the Magical Symbolism of Iron Working." 2003. *Folklore*, Vol. 114, No. 3, 427–433.

Lykiardopoulos, Amica. "The Evil Eye: Towards an Exhaustive Study." 1981. *Folklore*, Vol. 92, No. 2, 221–230.

Matin, Peyman. "Apotropaic Plants in Persian Folk Culture." 2012. *Iran & the Caucasus*, Vol. 16, No. 2, 189–200.

Nunio, Anton Alvar. 2012. "Ocular Pathologies and the Evil Eye in the Early Roman Principate." *Numen*, Vol. 59, No. 4, 295–321.

Refaey, Kim, G. C. Quinones, William Clifton, et al. "The Eye of Horus: The Connection Between Art, Medicine and Mythology in Ancient Egypt." 2019. *Cureus.*

Reminick, Ronald A. "The Evil Eye Belief Among the Amhara of Ethiopia." 1974. *Ethnology*, Vol. 13, No. 3, 279–291.

Ross, Colin Andrew. "The Electrophysiological Basis of the Evil Eye Belief." 2010. *Anthropology of Consciousness*, Vol. 21, Issue 1, 47–57.

Roussou, Eugenia. "Believing in the Supernatural through the 'Evil Eye': Perception and Science in the Modern Greek Cosmos." 2014. *Journal of Contemporary Religion*, Vol. 29, No. 3, 425–438.

Sagiv, Gadi. "Dazzling Blue: Color Symbolism, Kabbalistic Myth, and the Evil Eye in Judaism." 2017. *Numen*, Vol. 64, No. 2/3, 183–208.

Secunda, Shai. "The Fractious Eye: On the Evil Eye of Menstruants in Zoroastrian Tradition." 2014. *Numen*, Vol. 61, No. 1, 83–108.

Selare, R. "A Collection of Saliva Superstitions." 1939. *Folklore*, Vol. 50, No. 4, 349–366.

Thomsen, Marie-Louise. "The Evil Eye in Mesopotamia." 1992. *Journal of Near Eastern Studies*, Vol. 51, No. 1, 19–32.

ONLINE RESOURCES

Bible.com
Chabad.org
Christianitytoday.com
Jewishvirtuallibrary.org
Learn-islam.org
Metmuseum.org
Myjewishlearning.com
Oca.org
Pewresearch.org
Philamuseum.org
sacred-texts.com
sefaria.org
Wildhunt.org
Zoroastrians.net

ACKNOWLEDGMENTS

My heartfelt thanks to Judika Illes, editor extraordinaire, who championed this book from idea to proposal to completed manuscript and offered wise counsel along the way. Working with Judika has been a magical journey and a dream come true!

The team at Red Wheel Weiser has been a joy to work with. My thanks to Peter Turner, Kathryn Sky-Peck, Gia Manalio-Bonaventura, Jane Hagaman, Sylvia Hopkins, and Brittany Criag. A tip of the hat to copyeditor R. Nagengast, for her excellent eagle eye and direction.

I spoke to and interviewed many scholars and academics throughout the writing of this book. Some requested to remain anonymous, but you know who you are, and I thank you for your time. I also extend my gratitude to Sabina Magliocco, PhD; Alireeza Doostdar, PhD; Gideon Bohak, PhD; Ido Noy, PhD; Jennifer Houser Wegner, PhD; Eliseo Torres, PhD; and Christopher A. Faraone, PhD, for answering my many questions with professionalism and enthusiasm. A special note of thanks to Ronald Hutton, D.Phil. who generously offered his wisdom on other esoteric subjects I've written about in recent years.

I have been blessed with many teachers, and I am grateful for their wisdom and inspiration, whether I garnered it via their books or through personal friendships: Leo Louis Martello (whom I met a few years after he died), Lori Bruno, Margot Adler (who so generously granted me an interview when I was in college, and whose advice and warm words I will hold in my heart forever), Christopher Penczak, Laurie Cabot, Penny Cabot, Judika Illes (yes, again), Ivo Dominguez, Jr., Phyllis Curott, Rachel Pollack, and Denise Alvarado.

I thank my family, who support me at every turn: my husband, Michael, for always being the best; my sister, Maria, brother-in-law, David, and my incredibly brilliant and beautiful niece, Chloe Rose; my brother, Joseph; my aunt, Antoinette, and her husband, Mike; and my parents, Rosa and Nunzio. (Like every Italian son, I owe a particularly big hug to my mother, who always has the best advice). To my other family just across the Hudson River: Bob, Jody, Barry, Kim and the always adorable Evan and Hannah.

Rabbis Rolando Matalon and Felicia Sol of Temple B'nai Jeshurun, for their wisdom, insights, and cherished influence in our lives.

It was a tremendous blessing to interview several spiritual leaders while I was writing this book—Catholic priests, Eastern Orthodox priests, Imams, and other priests and priestesses who wish to remain anonymous. I offer each of you my heartfelt thanks.

My colleagues at The Wild Hunt continue to support my reporting on the pagan and magical communities, and I thank them for cheering me on: Manny Tejada, Eric O. Scott, Stacy Psaros, and especially Star Bustamonte, who is a star indeed!

Special thanks to my friend, Sophia, who honors the tradition and knows the magic.

Jessica Pimentel, my friend of many lifetimes, became a part of the journey of this book, and for that I am truly grateful.

For assisting me daily, I thank St. Therese of Lisieux (for the roses), Archangel Michael, St. Anthony of Padua, Marie Laveau, Papa Legba, Hekate, and Diana.

With love and respect I honor the ancestors who continue to influence my life as a magical practitioner, especially my maternal grandparents, Giuseppe and Caterina.

ABOUT THE AUTHOR

Antonio Pagliarulo writes regularly about spirituality, witchcraft, and paganism, and the intersection of folk magic with popular culture and religion. He has been published by the *Washington Post*, *NBC News*, the *New York Daily News*, *Religion News Service*, and *The Wild Hunt*. The son of Italian immigrants, Antonio had been schooled since childhood in the ways of Italian folk magic. As such, his practice draws from paganism, Roman Catholicism, Evil Eye magic, and the tarot. Antonio holds a BA in sociology from Purchase College, State University of New York. He lives in New York City.

Visit him online at *www.antoniopagliarulo.com*.

TO OUR READERS